God Demands Obedience

When We Obey God, We Can Be Sure He Will Keep His Promises.

Brenda M. Puckett

with James E. Puckett Sr.

Dedication

I, Brenda, dedicate this book to my mother, who is in Heaven. She always taught me not to take shortcuts in life, but to do what was right. Most importantly, she always taught me the importance of obedience in my walk with God. I, James, also dedicate this book to my mother and father who are both in Heaven. They demanded obedience in the home and taught me the importance of obeying righteous authority at all levels, especially godly authority.

Contents

Introduction

As we discuss the subject of obedience and its meaning, it brings back many memories of all the times in both of our lives when we were disobedient both as a married couple and in our individual lives. But even looking back at our childhood days, we remember how our parents demanded obedience from us. For this book, we will be using the King James Version (KJV) of Scripture for all quotes unless otherwise noted.

We are sure that you too can recall times when you as a child did not obey your parents, teacher, or some other authority figure. No child growing up wants to be labeled as disobedient. Moreover, the Bible clearly states what will happen when children don't honor and obey their parents (Ephesians 6:1; Colossians 3:20).

You might be asking, "Why is obedience so important?" We believe it's important because our lives can be summed up in one of two ways: either as obeying what we are told to do or doing what we want to do. When we say, "obeying what we are told to do," we are talking about what the Word of God has instructed us to do and the leading and instruction of the Holy Spirit.

Furthermore, the Bible has a lot to say about obedience. In the New Testament, the word "obedience" appears twelve times. The word "obedient" appears eight times in the Old Testament and eight times in the New Testament. The word "obey" appears forty-three times in the Old Testament and twenty-six times in the New Testament. Likewise, the word "obeyed" appears thirty-four times in the Old Testament and seven times in the New Testament. Clearly, the Bible has much to say about obedience. Let's discuss some examples.

The Bible instructs children to obey their parents (Ephesians 6:1; Colossians 3:20). It instructs Christians to obey those that have rule over us (Hebrews 13:17). In Ephesian 5:21, husbands and wives are instructed to submit to each other. In Ephesian 5:22, the wife is told to submit herself unto her husband, and in Ephesians 6:5, those who serve are instructed to obey those who are master of or have authority over them. Even though the word "submit" is used at times, it has the same meaning as the word "obey". We understand that some of these things can be difficult to talk about, but it is vitally important that we do. We will expand more on these Scriptures later in the book.

The Bible is also full of the promises of God, but they are all based on conditions. Those conditions are whether we obey His Word or disobey His Word. If we obey and do what He has told us to do, we receive His promises. Likewise, if we disobey and refuse to do what He has told us, then we don't get to enjoy His promises.

Whenever obedience is discussed, it is hard not to talk about disobedience. Disobedience is the opposite of obedience. In this book, we will place our attention on obedience because that's what we desire to be. No one wants to be known as a disobedient person. Being labeled as disobedient is like having "Rebellious" tattooed on your forehead.

One place that demands obedience is the military. We both served, so we understand what a command is and what it requires of the person to whom the command is issued. When we were commanded to carry out a task, we had better do it, or else. We had an option to either do what we were told or to disobey. If we did it, then there was no punishment. If we didn't do it, then there was punishment.

Likewise, God's commands are not optional. If they were, they would not be called commands. In the military, commands were not suggestions: if we felt like it, if we wanted to, or if we had time. No! It meant we did what we were told or suffered the consequences. It's no different when it comes to God's commands. The Bible is a book filled with commands from God. His commands are not to be replaced with our way of thinking, and our way of thinking is not a substitute for the Word of God. Look at Isaiah:

> Let the wicked forsake his way, and the unrighteous man his thoughts: and let him return unto the Lord, and he will have mercy upon him; and to our God, for he will abundantly pardon. For my thoughts are not your thoughts, neither are your ways my ways, saith the Lord. For as the heavens are higher than the earth, so are my ways higher than your ways, and my thoughts than your thoughts (Isaiah 55:7-9).

Obedience is for every person. No one is exempt from obeying something or someone. Obedience makes up the majority of our lives. Now that we have a better understanding of the importance of obedience, it is equally as important to understand what obedience means. In the New Strong's Complete Dictionary of Bible Words, the English word "obedience" is "Nawkay" (5218) or "Nawkaw" (5217) in Hebrew. From those Hebrew words, we get the definition "afflicted, broken, stricken, and wounded." We find these words in Isaiah 53, where Isaiah is prophesying about how Jesus would one day obey His Father and submit His life as a ransom for humanity.

Likewise, the Greek word for "obedience" is "Hupakoe," which comes from the word "Hupakouo," which means: to listen attentively; to heed or conform to a command or authority; and to hearken, be obedient to, and obey. As used in Hebrews 5:9, the Greek word translates to "submit, obey, and be obedient to God." We also see this same Greek word used in the book of Romans. It says, "For as by one man's disobedience many were made sinners, so by the obedience of one shall many be made righteous" (Romans 5:19). This verse speaks directly to Jesus' obedience, offering His life so that you and I could be saved.

As we can see, the words "obedience, obedient, obey, and submit" have intertwined meanings. They fit together like hand and glove. As you can imagine, we cannot cover everything that the Bible has to say about the subject of obedience. However, our hope is that after reading this book, you will realize how important obedience is to God and the benefits you can gain from it.

We have experienced the rewards of obeying God as well as the consequences of disobeying God both as individuals and as husband and wife. We can truly testify that the Scripture is correct when it says, "We ought to obey God rather than man" (Acts 5:29). As we share some of our personal stories as well as stories from the Bible to support our stance on obedience to God and to His Word, we hope that you will begin to live according to God's Word rather than trying to do it yourself. Maybe there are things that you need to stop trying to do your way and start submitting yourself to God's way instead. Regardless, we hope that you enjoy this book and that you will learn something you can apply to your own life as it relates to obeying God.

Brenda: Shortly before my mother passed away, one of my siblings asked her, "Why did you whip us so much?" She replied, "So you would obey." That was 17 years ago but those words still resonate with me today. I am a strong proponent of obedience and felt strongly in my heart to write a book on the topic. My husband suggested we write it together, and so we have. We hope it will bless you.

I have been saved for many years now and have seen God's promises manifest in my life over the years. But like most people, especially Christians, many of God's promises fulfilled in my life were all because I was willing to obey what the Bible says. As I became more mature in my walk with Jesus Christ, I experience some good things in my life. But I also had some bad things happen in my life just as we all do.

At first, I didn't discern the contrast between my good results to obeying God and my bad results to disobeying God. You have heard the term, "School of Hard Knocks." That was me. Most of the time it was my way or the highway. I was trying to do things my way and not the way the Bible says I should do it. After many disappointments and setbacks, I decided to try it God's way. It's sad to say but sometimes the only way we can learn to obey God is through our disobedience. The Bible say that Jesus learned obedience by the things He suffered (Hebrews 5:8). It's not that God wants us to suffer or that He is causing the suffering. We sometimes suffer the consequences of our own disobedience or the disobedience of others.

After I was filled with the Holy Spirit with the evidence of speaking in other tongues, I started to see the Word of God in a different light. I began to read my Bible more and seek God through prayer. I began to see my life changing for the better before my eyes. I knew it was a direct result of obeying God's Word and ceasing to do things my way. I started to do things God's way.

I began to see God for who He is and that He will do what He said. Look at Hebrews:

> But without faith it is impossible to please
> him: for he that cometh to God must believe
> that he is, and that he is a rewarder of them
> that diligently seek him (Hebrews 11:6).

When you believe that God is who He says He is, it will open the door to obeying Him. How could you obey someone or something that you don't trust or believe? We must trust and believe in God and His Word. As Scripture says, "Trust in the Lord with all thine heart; and lean not unto thine own understanding. In all thy ways acknowledge him, and he shall direct thy paths" (Proverbs 3:5-6). Trusting this way is the purest form of obedience a person can live by.

Samuel Johnson said, "He that hopes to find peace by trusting God must obey him." Trusting God is the prerequisite to obeying God. When we obey God, we find peace in our relationship with Him.

Chapter I
Rewards of Obeying God

Obedience shows God that we trust and love him. This gives us access to activate His power in our lives. He also wants to reward us for being obedient. When we talk about being rewarded by God for our obedience, what we are striving for is to please God. Everything we do in life should be to please Him. We please God by operating in faith, and that's when we are rewarded (Hebrews 11:6).

Moreover, God desires His children to be successful in every area of their life. Success comes from Him and not from the world. He wants His children to accomplish what He created them to be, and the only way to do so is to follow His plans and obey Him. As a result, success will manifest in our lives. After all, He didn't create us to be experts. If we are planning on accomplishing God's will in our lives, we must *do* according to His will. That means obeying and submitting our life to His ways, not our own.

The Bible speaks about great men who obeyed God and great men who disobeyed God. There is a story in the Bible about a man named Saul. He was serving as King over Israel, but he would make two major mistakes by being disobedient. Let's look at 1 Samuel:

> And some of the Hebrews went over Jordan
> to the land of Gad and Gilead. As for Saul,
> he was yet in Gilgal, and all the people
> followed him trembling. And he tarried
> seven days, according to the set time that
> Samuel had appointed: but Samuel came not

to Gilgal; and the people were scattered from him. And Saul said, Bring hither a burnt offering to me, and peace offerings. And he offered the burnt offering (1 Samuel 13:7-9).

Samuel was a prophet, and his job was to hear from God, then relay God's Word to King Saul and the people. When you read this story, you will discover that the prophet Samuel was not happy with Saul's decisions. Saul and Samuel had agreed that Saul would wait for Samuel to come to Gilgal. When he arrived, Samuel would offer suitable sacrifices to seek the Lord's help for victory over the Philistines. The instructions that Samuel gave to Saul were from God, but he got tired of waiting for Samuel and went against their agreement, Saul took a position of power by performing the role of the priest. He gathered and offered the burnt offerings from the people to God. (1 Samuel 13:9). As Samuel and Saul met, Samuel realized that Saul had disobeyed him and asked, "What have you done?" (1 Samuel 13:10).

Saul did not stop there. He disobeyed God a second time. Let's look at 1 Samuel again:

> Thus saith the Lord of hosts, I remember that which Amalek did to Israel, how he laid wait for him in the way, when he came up from Egypt. Now go and smite Amalek, and utterly destroy all that they have, and spare them not; but slay both man and woman, infant and suckling, ox and sheep, camel and ass (1 Samuel 15:2-3).

King Saul had clear and concise instructions about what to do and what not to do. After defeating Moab, Ammon, and

Edon in a major battle, King Saul was instructed by God, through the prophet Samuel, to go to war against the Amalekites. He was to kill everyone and everything. You might ask, "Why would God order such a thing?" Remember, in verse 2, God did not approve of what Amalek did to Israel, so God's vengeance was ordered against the Amalekites.

It was the Amalekites that first attacked the Israelites after they left Egypt (Exodus 17:8; Numbers 14:45). Even though the Israelites defeated the Amalekites during this battle, they continued to trouble the Israelites any way they could. They were described as a nation having no fear of the Lord. Moses would pronounce a curse from God on the Amalekites. He said that the Israelites would return to destroy the Amalekites after they had settled in the Promised Land. Look at Deuteronomy:

> Therefore it shall be, when the Lord thy God
> hath given thee rest from all thine enemies
> round about, in the land which the Lord thy
> God giveth thee for an inheritance to possess
> it, that thou shalt blot out the remembrance
> of Amalek from under heaven; thou shalt not
> forget it (Deuteronomy 25:19).

God was keeping His promise through King Saul and his army.

As a side note, at the very moment we are writing this book, Israel is engaged in an all-out bloody war with neighboring enemies. We can see from the above Scripture just how much God has loved and still loves Israel. God promised to make Israel a great nation, to bless it, and to make its name great. He also promised to bless those who bless Israel and to curse those who disfavor Isarel. God promised that all the families of the earth would be blessed if we bless Israel (Genesis 12:1-3). In the Old Testament, Israel is alluded to as God's vineyard and as His sons (Isaiah 5:7; Jeremiah 6:9; Hosea. 10:1). The Bible also tells us to pray for Israel (Psalm 122:6). God even called Israel His firstborn (Exodus 4:22). So, do you think God cares about Israel? I'd say He does.

Clearly, God is serious about Israel. When He gave the order for Saul to destroy the Amalekites and leave nothing behind, He was not playing. When God tells us to do something, we had better obey His orders. Saul was obedient in attacking the Amalekites just as Samuel instructed, but he was disobedient by letting King Agag and all the animals live. Not only did Saul disobey the Word of the Lord, but he also lied to Samuel and told him that he had done what he was told to do.

King Saul failed to learn a valuable lesson. He did not realize that to obey is better than sacrifice (1 Samuel 15:22). He was attempting to right his wrong by sacrificing the fat of a ram. King Saul only obeyed part of God's instructions, and because of his disobedience he was ripped of his kingship. Look at 1 Samuel again:

> And Samuel said unto him, The Lord hath
> rent the kingdom of Israel from thee this day,
> and hath given it to a neighbour of thine, that
> is better than thou (1 Samuel 15:28).

If we want to please God and desire His blessings in our lives, we must obey Him and do exactly what He has asked of us. Partial obedience does not please God. God is our Heavenly Father, who is full of wealth, favor, and prosperity.

To receive everything He has promised, we must first obey His commands in full order.

The lessons to take away from Saul's disobedience towards God are: (1) It is always better to obey God than to make sacrifices for our own agendas, and (2) God calls us to submit to *His* will and not *our* will (1 Samuel 15:22). After Saul's failures, God changed his position for his disobedient actions. Saul also admitted that he had sinned but blamed the people for it (1 Samuel 15:24). We could say that Saul feared the people more than he feared God.

Almost every time we talk about obeying God, we quote only part of the Scripture from 1 Samuel 15:22, which is, "To obey is better than sacrifice." However, we rarely connect it to our giving. Let us explain. In Saul's case, God instructed him, through His prophet Samuel, to take certain actions. Saul disobeyed, and then tried to appease God by giving Him an offering that He never asked for.

As Christians, we sometimes try to please God by giving and offering our money to make up for our disobedience towards Him. We are not saying you should withhold offerings. In fact, we encourage you to give your money, but giving a money offering will never replace obedience or be a form of immunity for disobedience.

Furthermore, when we *are* ready to give an offering of our money, we should ask God what He would have us give. I think we do not ask Him because we are afraid of what He might tell us to give. God already knows what we can give. He will never tell you to give an amount that you do not have.

The next offering time at your church, before you give the same twenty-dollar bill you give every Sunday, take a few minutes to ask God what amount He would have you give. When He tells you, obey Him in giving that amount, and watch your blessing unfold right before your eyes.

A.W. Tozer said, "The Bible recognizes no faith that does not lead to obedience, nor does it recognize any obedience that does not spring from faith. The two are at opposite sides of the same coin."

Chapter II
Disobedience is of The Flesh

Have you ever felt that God was calling you to do something you didn't want to? You thought of every excuse why you couldn't. Unfortunately, excuses do not exempt us from the results of our decision to obey or disobey. Many times, the excuses we make come from our flesh. We can only operate in the Spirit or in the flesh, but obedience to God can only be accomplished by walking in the Spirit.

The Bible tells us to put our flesh to shame or to humiliate it if we desire to obey God and prevent His anger towards us (Colossians 3:5-6). If we allow our flesh or members of our flesh to rule over us, we will find it hard to obey God.

As we grew in Christ, we came to understand that obedience can come in the form of a test from God. God will evaluate our obedience toward Him. These are the times when we can learn much about ourselves. When we are challenged to a test, God is waiting to see if we are going to obey Him or if we are going to do it another way. The only safe and sure way is doing it God's way.

Passing God's tests in our lives should be something that every Christian desires. Unfortunately, this is not always the case. Often, we fail the test because we do not have faith in what He is instructing us to do. As we discussed before, we can only please God through our faith (Hebrews 11:6). If we do not believe and have faith, how can we submit, or obey? When this happens, we find ourselves like the children of Israel, going around and around the mountain. Let's look at Moses from the Bible.

Moses was the Hebrew prophet who led the children of Israel out of Egypt. God told Moses that He would use him to deliver His people out of the hands of Pharaoh (Exodus 3). After much dialogue with God, and after God had given him sign after sign, Moses obeyed God. Look at Exodus:

> Now therefore, behold, the cry of the children of Israel is come unto me: and I have also seen the oppression wherewith the Egyptians oppress them. Come now therefore, and I will send thee unto Pharaoh, that thou mayest bring forth my people the children of Israel out of Egypt (Exodus 3:9-10).

There Moses received his commission from God. But even after God assured him and gave him many signs, Moses still did not obey God's instructions. When the people were journeying through the wilderness and started to complain, Moses took it upon himself to please the people. Look at Exodus again:

> Wherefore the people did chide with Moses, and said, Give us water that we may drink. And Moses said unto them, Why chide ye with me? wherefore do ye tempt the Lord? And the people thirsted there for water; and the people murmured against Moses, and said, Wherefore is this that thou hast brought us up out of Egypt, to kill us and our children and our cattle with thirst? And Moses cried unto the Lord, saying, What shall I do unto this people? they be almost ready to stone me. And the Lord said unto Moses, Go on before the people, and take with thee of the

elders of Israel; and thy rod, wherewith thou
smotest the river, take in thine hand, and go.
Behold, I will stand before thee there upon
the rock in Horeb; and thou shalt smite the
rock, and there shall come water out of it,
that the people may drink. And Moses did so
in the sight of the elders of Israel (Exodus
17:2-6).

The above verses tell us that while in the wilderness, the
children of Israel complained to Moses about their thirst and
their animals' thirst. Moses took the people's complaints to
the Lord, and the Lord instructed Moses what to do. God
told Moses to take the rod he was carrying and hit the rock
of Horeb with it. Remember, this was the same rod God had
used to demonstrate His power to Moses before. Moses
obeyed the Lord, and the rock produced water.

When we obey God, we can expect to receive what God has
promised. But when we disobey God, we can also expect to
receive the consequences of our disobedience Now that we
have seem what happened with Moses when he obeyed God,
in contrast, let's see what happened when Moses disobeyed
God. Look at Numbers:

Take the rod, and gather thou the assembly
together, thou, and Aaron thy brother, and
speak ye unto the rock before their eyes; and
it shall give forth his water, and thou shalt
bring forth to them water out of the rock: so
thou shalt give the congregation and their
beasts drink. And Moses took the rod from
before the Lord, as he commanded him. And
Moses and Aaron gathered the congregation
together before the rock, and he said unto

them, Hear now, ye rebels; must we fetch you water out of this rock? And Moses lifted up his hand, and with his rod he smote the rock twice: and the water came out abundantly, and the congregation drank, and their beasts also. And the Lord spake unto Moses and Aaron, Because ye believed me not, to sanctify me in the eyes of the children of Israel, therefore ye shall not bring this congregation into the land which I have given them (Numbers 20:8-12).

In the verses before the passage of Scripture above, we find the Israelites complaining to Moses again. So, Moses and Aaron went before the Lord again with the complaints of the people. So far, Moses was doing everything right. He was smart to seek God for an answer to the people's complaint. But Moses missed it when he took the rod and struck the rock. Once again, this is the same rod God had been using to supply the people and the animals with water. He struck it not once, but twice.

I think Moses thought he was doing God a favor, but God had never instructed Moses to hit the rock at all in this situation. Rather, Moses was told to *speak* to the rock. But God, in His mercy and sovereignty, would not disappoint the people, even though Moses had done what he wanted instead of submitting to the will of God. Therefore, when Moses struck the rock twice, water did still come forth.

Mose was clearly operating in his flesh. Imagine the people complaining and murmuring to Moses about not having water and other necessities during their journey in the wilderness. Moses probably figured that if striking the rock worked the first time, why wouldn't it work again? I think any average leader would have done the same thing as Moses. He thought he was doing the right thing for the people. Moses most likely lost his temper over their whining and struck the rock twice to make a point before giving the people water. Moses allowed his flesh to overrule what God had instructed him to do. The Bible says for us to walk in the Spirit, and by doing so, we won't fulfill the lust of the flesh (Galatians 5:16).

Because of Moses disobedience, he was not allowed to take the children of Isarel into the Promised Land. Numbers 20:12, reads "And the Lord spake unto Moses and Aaron, Because ye believed me not, to sanctify me in the eyes of the children of Israel, therefore ye shall not bring this congregation into the land which I have given them." Imagine how Moses must have felt about God's decision. After all that time in the wilderness, with a group of ungrateful people, he isn't even granted the grand finale—a place that flows with milk and honey.

Moses brought this upon himself. You might say, "Well, it wasn't his fault. It's the people's fault." No! It was all Moses' fault. Moses was given clear instructions and concise information beforehand, at the very moment he sought God. Moses had no one to blame but himself.

Many times, we are like Moses. We can do everything right, to a certain point. We can obey God about one thing but disobey Him about another. If Moses, one of the greatest, if not the greatest leader in Jewish history received this type of punishment for his disobedience, imagine the potential consequences for our disobedience.

Peter Bulkeley said, "If God be God over us, we must yield him universal obedience in all things. He must not be over us in one thing, and under us in another, but he must be over us in everything."

We might not be commissioned by God to lead a group of people from captivity, but we are all called by God to do *something*. Our rewards are found in our obedience to do what we are called to do. And just like Moses, making excuses like we are not qualified or cannot do it are not grounds for immunity from the outcome of our disobedience.

Doing What's Right When Everyone Else is Doing Wrong

Obedience is easy when everyone around us is being obedient. It's much easier to do the same thing as the people around us, even if it's wrong. In fact, we have the tendency to side with whatever the majority is ruling in most situations. But as Christians, we must draw the line when it comes to doing what's right. Doing what's right in all circumstances requires obedience. There will come a time when we as Christians will have to choose between obedience and disobedience.

Christians must separate themselves from those that choose not to obey God's Word. Sometimes peer pressure can be a leading force for disobedience, especially amongst young people. If we find ourselves in the middle of a people who are disobeying the Word of God, we as Christians must not side with them. This requires a total commitment to obedience.

It's easy to tell if a Christian is sold out to God or is just testing the water. Obedience to God in every area of life and in all circumstances is non-wavering. Choosing to obey God's Word and submit to His will over our will is the narrow way. Going along with the crowd is taking the broad way, which leads to destruction (Matthew 7:13-14).

Chapter III
Disobedience and the Heart

You might not expect this, but the heart can cause us to be disobedient towards God. When a person's heart is not right, he is not willing to do anything the Lord has instructed him to do. This is why we must be a person who seeks the heart of God (1 Samuel 13:14; Acts 13:22). When we desire what God desires, we will obey Him.

We all know what the word "heart" means from a medical standpoint. But what about from a spiritual standpoint? In the New Testament, the word "heart" in the Greek is "kardia (2588)," which means the thoughts or feelings (your mind) and the middle. The heart of man is where life's decisions are made. It is that place where we decide to obey God or not. The Bible commands us to keep and guard our hearts because the heart is where disobedience or obedience flows from (Proverbs 4:23). Jeremiah 17:9 explains that the heart is deceitful and wicked, and we don't even know it. It's from the heart that we say what we are going to do or not going to do (Matthew 12:34).

It is vitally important for us to love what God loves and hate what God hates. Without doing this, disobedience will be the outcome of all our decisions. Enough disobedience will lead to a hardened heart. With a hardened heart, we cannot obey God's Word or what He asks us to do. If our heart is about anything other than doing the *will* of God, we will not obey Him.

In Jesus' first sermon, what we call the Sermon on the Mount, He told us a lot about the heart in just a few words. Look at Matthew:

> Blessed are the pure in heart: for they shall
> see God (Matthew 5:8).

The phrase "Pure in heart" tells it all. To be pure in heart means to be real and authentic in our walk with the Lord, not fake. To be pure in heart is to be honest with God. We can't hide anything from Him. This means that when we sin, we repent. When someone does us wrong, we forgive them. When God tells us to do something, we do it without hesitation or complaining. Disobedience is not found in a pure-hearted person.

The Bible warns us that our heart can become disobedient toward God by falling into unbelief. We have already been warned about guarding our hearts because from it flows the issues of life (Proverbs 4:23). Because of the heart's importance, the writer of Hebrews issues a stern warning. Let's look at it.

> Take care, brothers and sisters, that there not
> be in any one of you a wicked, unbelieving
> [a]heart [which refuses to trust and rely on
> the Lord, a heart] that turns away from the
> living God. But continually encourage one
> another every day, as long as it is called
> "Today" [and there is an opportunity], so that
> none of you will be hardened [into settled
> rebellion] by the deceitfulness of sin [its
> cleverness, delusive glamour, and
> sophistication] (Hebrews 3:12-13, Amplified
> Bible).

An unbelieving heart will cause us to miss out on the blessing God has promised us. In the passage of Scripture above, we are told to "Take care." Other translations use the words "Watch out," "Be careful," "Be attentive," "Take heed," and "Beware." These are verb adjectives that compel us to hear, submit, and obey. These are the same words we discussed in our definition of the Greek word used for obedience, "Hupakoe." When we are given the opportunity to obey God, we should be quick to do so, because if we don't watch out, unbelief can creep in and cause disobedience. An unbelieving heart that is disobedient to God will cause you to fall away from the faith, but we are not talking about losing your salvation as far as going to Heaven. This is about not just being a Christian but being an obedient Christian.

Our job is to do what the Bible tells us to do. Will we always get it right? No! But as believers, we are to find out the *will* of God for our lives and be willing to live it out to the best of our ability through obeying His Word.

Disobedience Causes a Hardened Heart

We talked a lot about the heart. There is much to be said about the heart of man because it is the core operation center of man's existence. The Bible has a lot to say about the hardening of the heart. This is something that happens to us when we decide to not obey God. Every time we disobey God, our heart becomes a little harder. The harder our heart becomes, the more we stop believing God's Word and rebel against His commandments. Because God gives each of us free will, He will allow the disobedience in our life to harden our hearts. This is not something that He desires for us, but

He will let us make our own decisions. A passage of Scripture comes to mind about just how easy it is for us to harden our hearts. Let's look at Romans:

> Because that, when they knew God, they glorified him not as God, neither were thankful; but became vain in their imaginations, and their foolish heart was darkened. Professing themselves to be wise, they became fools, And changed the glory of the uncorruptible God into an image made like to corruptible man, and to birds, and fourfooted beasts, and creeping things. Wherefore God also gave them up to uncleanness through the lusts of their own hearts, to dishonour their own bodies between themselves: Who changed the truth of God into a lie, and worshipped and served the creature more than the Creator, who is blessed for ever. Amen. For this cause God gave them up unto vile affections: for even their women did change the natural use into that which is against nature: And likewise also the men, leaving the natural use of the woman, burned in their lust one toward another; men with men working that which is unseemly, and receiving in themselves that recompence of their error which was meet. And even as they did not like to retain God in their knowledge, God gave them over to a reprobate mind, to do those things which are not convenient; (Romans 1:21-28).

This is a long passage of Scripture, but it is a good illustration of how our heart can become hard. When we stop believing the Word of God, it results in a cycle of glorifying people or things and not God. As a result of this, our way of thinking will become meaningless. When we stop believing what God has said and stop doing what God said, our heart starts becoming hard. We can never be satisfied outside of God's *will* for our life.

The passage of Scripture above is talking about sexual idolatry, but any kind of idolatry will harden the heart. Disobedience is disobedience. It doesn't matter what area it's used in. Anytime we decide to trade God and His Word for what we believe to be more satisfying, it becomes an idol. When idols creep into our life, we start to become disobedient and disregard everything God has said. God's answer to their idolatry was to give them up to do whatever they felt like doing and to let them feel however they felt like feeling. But God didn't stop there. He gave them over to a reprobate mind. At this stage, all self-restraint to do the right thing is gone. There is nothing left to make us want to obey God. Our heart has become hard towards God and everything He says. This is a bad place to be. When God gives us over and gives us up, watch out, because we are in for a rough ride on life.

When God takes His hand off us, we have a mind of our own to do and say whatever we feel like, and all the time think we are doing what's right. As it says in verse 21, our hearts become darkened. One of the ways our heart becomes dark is from disobedience. And a disobedient heart becomes a hardened heart. Don't get on God's bad side and cause Him to give you up and give you over.

If Jesus is our Lord, and He is, then we should give Him total control over our lives. This does not mean that we are not allowed to freely live our lives and make our own decisions. When we say, "Jesus is our Lord and Savior," we are saying, "We obey Him, and He's our salvation." Sadly, many people want to have it one way. We can live our whole life and make Jesus our Savior, but refuse to make Him our Lord. When we do this long enough, He will remove His hand from our lives. This is another sober message about the importance of obedience. If we live our life according to the Bible and obey what it says, we can live free of a hardened heart.

Obedience is a Condition of *Will*

> And if it seem evil unto you to serve the Lord, choose you this day whom ye will serve; whether the gods which your fathers served that were on the other side of the flood, or the gods of the Amorites, in whose land ye dwell: but as for me and my house, we will serve the Lord (Joshua 24:15).

Obedience is a choice just like disobedience is a choice. Like Joshua, every person must make up their own mind whether he is going to obey God or disobey God. Using Joshua's perspective on choosing to serve the Lord, each one of us have a choice to obey or disobey the Lord. Every Christian confession should be, "As for me and my house, we *will* obey the Lord" or "As for me and my life, I *will* obey the Lord."

Let's look at some examples from the Bible of how people's hearts were hardened because of their *willingness* to be disobedient and how God blessed them after they were *willing* to be obedient. As children, we both heard the story about this man name Jonah who was swallowed by a whale. The Bible does not say it was a whale, but rather a great fish (Jonah 1:17). We do know that this great fish was large enough to consume Jonah, but enough about the fish. Let's talk about Jonah.

Jonah was an Old Testament prophet whom God told to go to a city call Nineveh and preach repentance. Not much is said about Jonah outside of the Book of Jonah except for a mention of him in 2 Kings 14:25, where he is expressed as a servant of the Lord. Nevertheless, God chose to use him to reach the people in Nineveh. Let's look at Jonah:

> Now the word of the Lord came unto Jonah the son of Amittai, saying, Arise, go to Nineveh, that great city, and cry against it; for their wickedness is come up before me. But Jonah rose up to flee unto Tarshish from the presence of the Lord, and went down to Joppa; and he found a ship going to Tarshish: so he paid the fare thereof, and went down into it, to go with them unto Tarshish from the presence of the Lord (Jonah 1:1-3).

Jonah's first mistake was to think he could hide from God. This is a lesson for all of us. The Bible tells us that the earth and everything on it belongs to God (Psalms 21:1). That includes the people. There is no getting away from God no matter how hard we try. David gives details in the Book of Psalms about the omniscience and omnipresence of God (Psalms 139). So, for us to think we can run from Him, we are living with a hardened heart.

So, what did Jonah do to disobey God? The Scripture says that Jonah was ordered by God to go to Nineveh and warn them to repent and turn back to God. But Jonah had a plan of his own. Jonah decided to disobey God and do what he thought would get God off his back.

Jonah probably thought that he was not the one that God should call on to do such a job. Like many of us, when God tells us to do something and we think we are not the one to do it, we make excuses and say God must have made a mistake. God does not make mistakes.

Instead of obeying God and going to Nineveh, Jonah got on a ship and went in the opposite direction. Jonah didn't want to go anywhere close to Nineveh. He decided to go to Joppa because he didn't like what God had commanded him to do. Someone might ask, "Why would a servant of God refuse to obey God?" That's a good question, but we don't have a good answer for it. However, the Scripture does tell us why Jonah did not want to go it Nineveh.

Besides the fact that Jonah probably feared the people of Nineveh, the main reason Jonah disobeyed God is because he didn't want to preach to the people because he was afraid that they might repent and be forgiven. Look at Jonah again:

> But it displeased Jonah exceedingly, and he was very angry. And he prayed unto the Lord, and said, I pray thee, O Lord, was not this my saying, when I was yet in my country? Therefore I fled before unto Tarshish: for I knew that thou art a gracious God, and merciful, slow to anger, and of great kindness, and repentest thee of the evil. Therefore now, O Lord, take, I beseech thee, my life from me; for it is better for me to die

than to live. Then said the Lord, Doest thou
well to be angry? (Jonah 4:1-4).

Jonah's heart became hard amidst his disobedience. He wanted God to punish and destroy Nineveh. We think this is a valuable lesson for every one of us. When we disobey God, we turn our heart against God and His plan, whether that plan is for us or for some other person. God could be commanding us to go somewhere or do something, and we flat out refuse to comply with His command.

When we know that we are to witness to someone about leading them to Jesus, but we disobey and get our mouth shut, we are disobeying God. Bringing souls into His Kingdom is His will (1 Timothy 2:3-4). Leading someone to Christ is not something we have to wait for God to tell us to do. He has already told us to win souls and not to be ashamed of it (Luke 9:26). He could be telling us to witness to a family member or a close friend who has hurt us or done us wrong. Because we haven't forgiven them, we disobey God when He orders us to go to them, and because of our disobedience, our heart becomes hard. This is what happened to Jonah. So, Jonah tried to flee from the Lord (Jonah 1:3).

Jonah didn't like the fact that God wanted the people of Nineveh to repent, and that he was the one God chose to tell them. Jonah paid for a ticket to Tarshish (Jonah 1:3), but he ended up paying a whole lot more. It's no different when we disobey God. When we think we are outsmarting God, we can guarantee we will end up paying the most. Disobeying God by trying to run from Him will cost us our time, peace, health, money, and joy. All these things are found in doing what God has told us to do.

Let's examine a person in the Bible whose heart was hardened because of disobedience toward God. We have already discussed how Moses disobeyed God and what it cost him in the end. We now want to look at Pharaoh. God didn't speak directly to Pharaoh, but sent His servant, Moses, to do His bidding. Either way, God was commanding Pharaoh to do something, but he disobeyed God. Look at Exodus:

> And afterward Moses and Aaron went in, and told Pharaoh, Thus saith the Lord God of Israel, Let my people go, that they may hold a feast unto me in the wilderness. And Pharaoh said, Who is the Lord, that I should obey his voice to let Israel go? I know not the Lord, neither will I let Israel go. And they said, The God of the Hebrews hath met with us: let us go, we pray thee, three days' journey into the desert, and sacrifice unto the Lord our God; lest he fall upon us with pestilence, or with the sword (Exodus 5:1-3).

You can almost hear the arrogance in the Pharaoh's voice saying, "Who is the Lord that I should obey his voice to let Israel go?" Pharaoh was not the name of a certain person. A Pharaoh was a person who ruled the land of the Egyptians and was god over them. He was the king of Egypt during this time. It was the Pharaoh's way or no way. So, you can imagine when Moses and Aaron gave Pharaoh the news of what the Lord had said, he was not too pleased. After all, in his mind, he was the one and only god of the Egyptians. Pharaoh was about to find out who the real God was, though.

Pharaoh probably knew of many gods, but had never heard of the Lord that Moses and Aaron spoke off. So, without any further understanding, he refused and said, "No." Moses and Aaron tried to explain to Pharaoh what Lord they were acting on behalf of and what would happen if he disobeyed. We believe that if Pharaoh had taken the time to gain knowledge and understanding about who the Lord was, he would have let them go without hesitation.

Let's go back to chapter three of Exodus to see the Lord's first request to Pharaoh.

> And they shall hearken to thy voice: and thou shalt come, thou and the elders of Israel, unto the king of Egypt, and ye shall say unto him, The Lord God of the Hebrews hath met with us: and now let us go, we beseech thee, three days' journey into the wilderness, that we may sacrifice to the Lord our God (Exodus 3:18).

Pharaoh was commanded by the Lord to allow the people three days to worship Him. When the Lord made this request, He already knew that Pharaoh would disobey (Exodus 3:19). We believe this is the beginning stage of Pharaoh's heart being hardened. Every time we disobey God, our heart hardens further and further.

After Pharaoh refused the peoples' three-day leave, the Lord put Plan B into motion, which you can read about in chapter three and four of Exodus.

> And the Lord said unto Moses, When thou goest to return into Egypt, see that thou do all those wonders before Pharaoh, which I

have put in thine hand: but I will harden his heart, that he shall not let the people go (Exodus 4:21).

So, it was the Lord who hardened Pharaoh's heart. This is true. But it was a direct result of Pharaoh's disobedience toward the Lord. Look again at Exodus:

And he hardened Pharaoh's heart, that he hearkened not unto them; as the Lord had said. And the Lord said unto Moses, Pharaoh's heart is hardened, he refuseth to let the people go (Exodus 7:13-14).

Refusing to let the Lord's people go, caused Pharaoh to develop a hard heart. Pharaoh would not listen to what the Lord had said. Pharaoh's responses showed his arrogance. Imagine thinking that you know it all and not listening to and doing what the Lord tells you to do. It is not only arrogant, but prideful. Pharaoh caused this himself because of his disobedience in not complying with the Lord's commands. Because of his disobedience, the Lord's supernatural power was released against Egypt.

Now let's look at the consequences of Pharaoh's disobedience. First, his heart was hardened. Someone might ask, "Why was Pharaoh's heart hardened, and who did it?" These are great questions. Reading chapters seven, eight, and nine of Exodus gave us great insight into what was happening between Pharaoh and the Lord.

First, Pharaoh's heart was hardened because of his own stubbornness and his own bold disobedience toward God. We must understand that the kings or Pharaohs of Egypt were cruel and tyrant rulers of the Israelites. The Pharaohs' dictatorship over the Israelites had been going on for 400 years, and God was not pleased with their actions. These Pharaohs were so bad that at one point, it was ordered that all male babies be murdered at birth (Exodus 1:6). These were evil people.

Second, after Pharaoh realized that the Lord's punishment would not stop, he hardened his own heart by not letting the Israelites go. Look at Exodus 8:15, "But when Pharaoh saw that there was respite, he hardened his heart, and hearkened not unto them; as the Lord had said." Also, in verse 32, "But this time also Pharaoh hardened his heart" (Exodus 8:32). The Lord did harden Pharaoh's heart many times during the liberation of the Israelites and even after they had come out from Egypt (Exodus 14:4, 8, 17). One would think that God was setting Pharaoh up for the kill. You may say, "How could God do such a thing?" God knew that Pharaoh would not keep his word and obey Him. So, Pharaoh hardened his own heart by his repeated disobedience to God.

After reading and studying the back and forth of the Lord and Pharaoh, one can see that the Lord was giving Pharaoh a chance to do the right thing. It is also clear that Pharaoh might have been taunting the Lord because every time he said he would let the people go, he went back on his word.

God gave Pharaoh many warnings and chances to do the right thing, but he refused to obey. Because Pharaoh went against the Lord's commands, he brought further punishment on himself and the whole nation of Egypt. Once he realized that the plagues weren't going to stop, he dug his heels in out of defiance and pride and stood his ground against the Lord.

One would think Pharaoh would have come to understand and believe that the Lord was not playing around. After all, the dialogue between Pharaoh and Moses was about what the Lord would do if Pharaoh didn't let His people go. God followed up on every consequence he warned about. Pharaoh witnessed the stopping and starting of the plagues. When the plagues were visible, Pharaoh would comply with the Word of the Lord, but as soon as the plagues stopped, Pharaoh would enslave the people again.

We believe we all can learn from Pharaoh's disobedience. God is always trying to get us to obey Him. He knows it's in our best interest. Many times, when we are going through struggles, and it seems there is not relief, the first thing we tend to do is cry to God for help. Nevertheless, as soon as God answers us and spares us from our struggle, we tend to go back to our old ways of doing things. The Lord could have destroyed Pharoah at the beginning. Because God is merciful, he gave Pharaoh several chances to repent. God's patience with Pharaoh was meant to lead him to repentance (Romans 2:4), which He desires for us all.

Finally, Pharaoh came to himself and just couldn't take any more. He was ready to throw in the towel. He learned the hard way that he could not compete with the Lord. It took him a while, but he finally came to his senses. Look at this verse:

> And Pharaoh sent, and called for Moses and
> Aaron, and said unto them, I have sinned this
> time: the Lord is righteous, and I and my
> people are wicked (Exodus 9:27).

The last thing we will say about Pharaoh is this: he stood his ground as long as he could until the Lord got tired of his ways. The Lord's *will* shall be done. It doesn't matter how hard we fight and what we think, our *will* can never surpass the *will* of the Lord. It was the Lord's *will* to have Moses and Aaron deliver His people from the hands of Pharaoh, and that is exactly what He did.

Both Jonah's and Pharaoh's willingness to obey or disobey the Lord was a condition of their *will.* Our willingness to obey God will make all the different in His willingness to bless us. God is forever ready and willing to shower His children with His blessings.

Our Choices Have Consequences

Brenda: In 1990, my husband James, was serving a tour in Korea, and I went over to visit him for 30 days. James was very active in the local church he was attending. Every Sunday I was there, I went to church with him. One Sunday, I sensed the call of God to accept Him as my Lord and Savior, but I did not accept the call. I wasn't ready to give my life back to Him because I was still "straddling the fence," so to speak.

I had confessed Jesus Christ as my Lord and Savior when I was a young girl, around 11 or 12 years old. But as the years passed, somewhere along the way I had relieved Him of the title of "Lord" over my life. I knew, or at least thought, I was going to Heaven when I died, but I didn't want anything to do with Jesus having lordship over my life. I disobeyed Him in every way you can think of.

I was not aware of the Scripture that tells us that *today* is the day that we should get to know Him if we don't (2 Corinthians 6:2). My goal was to put off living for Jesus as long as I could. The Holy Spirit was tugging at my heart every day. I knew where the feelings that I was experiencing were coming from, but I wasn't ready to change.

I could see the change in my husband's life, but I wasn't ready to make that move yet. As time went on, I began to read the Bible and started praying. I had never heard of some of the things I was reading, but I understood enough to know that living for Him meant I must completely turn my life over to Him. I had to allow Jesus to be the Lord of my life and not just my Savior. It didn't happen right away, but when I decided to do it, I began to see the change in my life. The more I read the Bible, the more I obeyed Him. The more I obeyed Him, the more blessings were manifested in my life.

One day while reading in the Bible from the book of Deuteronomy, I read about how God would bless me if I obeyed Him, and the curses that would be upon my life if I disobeyed Him. It was clear that God wanted to bless me, but I was standing in the way by being disobedient. Let's look at Deuteronomy:

> Behold, I set before you this day a blessing and a curse; A blessing, if ye obey the commandments of the Lord your God, which I command you this day: And a curse, if ye will not obey the commandments of the Lord your God, but turn aside out of the way which I command you this day, to go after

other gods, which ye have not known (Deuteronomy 11:26-28).

It's important that we understand the ramifications of our choices. In the passage of Scripture above, God gave the people of Israel a choice: *Either you obey me, or you disobey me*. And whichever one they chose would determine whether they would be blessed or cursed, which would later unfold in their journey (Deuteronomy 11:29-30). Even after the people were warned about their choice of obedient or disobedient, Moses would continue to caution them to be sure to submit to everything the Lord had instructed them to do (Deuteronomy 11:32).

I think sometimes we must be reminded of the consequences of our decisions. Even though we are told what would happen if we disobeyed, we sometimes must be reminded. It is much harder to obey when we are always disobeying. To get to a place where we are comfortable in obeying the commandments of God, we must first trust Him and believe what He says. Blessings come from obedience, and curses come from disobedience. In the first chapter of Isaiah, he tells us the people of Judah's condition and how God gave them an ultimatum—to obey Him and receive the blessing or disobey Him and be cursed. Let's pick up Isaiah here:

> Learn to do well; seek judgment, relieve the oppressed, judge the fatherless, plead for the widow. Come now, and let us reason together, saith the Lord: though your sins be as scarlet, they shall be as white as snow; though they be red like crimson, they shall be as wool. If ye be willing and obedient, ye shall eat the good of the land: But if ye refuse

and rebel, ye shall be devoured with the sword: for the mouth of the Lord hath spoken it (Isaiah 1:17-19).

God gave the people a list of things that they were to do. If they obeyed Him, they would have plenty to eat. If they disobeyed Him, they would be destroyed. There's not much about this we don't understand. We obey, we are blessed. We disobey, we are cursed. In verse 19, Isaiah used the phrase, "Ye shall eat the good of the land." This would certainly mean everything that the land produced they would enjoy, i.e., vegetables, fruits, and everything in the way of food. But I believe eating the good of the land includes more than just physical food. I believe it means having all our needs supplied. The Bible says all that is on the earth, and everything and everyone that dwells on the earth belongs to the Lord (Psalm 24:1).

Then Isaiah gives the contrast to not obeying God. He tells the people that if they refuse and rebel against what the Lord has said, then they won't have to worry about receiving the blessings of God because they would not be around long enough to think about it. If they didn't repent and obey the Lord, they would be destroyed by the hand of the Babylonians. Judah would be burnt to the ground with nothing left (Isaiah 1:25).

Every time we choose sins over obedience, our hearts move towards God. When we continue to willfully disobey God after we know what it is He wants us to do, it becomes harder and harder for us to repent and surrender our disobedience for obedience. Look what Hebrews says:

<blockquote>
For there is no longer any sacrifice that will take away sins if we purposely go on sinning after the truth has been made known to us. Instead, all that is left is to wait in fear for the coming Judgment and the fierce fire which will destroy those who oppose God! (Hebrews 10:26-27, Good News Translation).
</blockquote>

This is what happens after a Christian continues to deliberately disobey God. The heart becomes defiant, which leads to a rebellious spirit. Their spirit becomes so rebellious against God that they say things like, "I don't care what the Bible says," or "God won't mind if I do it one more time." When we start to make excuses for our disobedience, it is time to have a serious talk with that person in the mirror. There must be a 180-degree turn in our behavior. It's time to turn from disobedience to obedience toward God.

Some people think they can clean themselves up. Granted, they must want to be clean and do the necessary things to become clean. But it's the Lord's job to clean them up. We don't have the power to destroy sin. Only God has that power.

I had a co-worker whose heart was bitter because of some things she was going through in life. She wanted to clean herself up and get things right with God. I kept telling her that Jesus was the only one that could cleanse her of her sins. She attended church from time to time and would be convicted by the Word of God, but showed no noticeable change in her behavior. God was showing her what she needed to correct in her life. The more she attended church, the more bitter she became. I knew what was happening and would talk to her about it as much as she would allow me. Because of her disobedience in not doing what she knew she had to do to stop feeling that way, she was developing a hardened heart.

There is an old proverb that says, "He that sins is human; he that grieves over sin is a saint; he that boasts of sin is of the devil; He that forgives sin is God. The heart and the eye are the agents of sin." I believe we all can relate to this proverb in some way or other. When God was pulling on my heart to live for Him, I was resisting Him at all costs. I was very aware of the actions I needed to take, but my heart would not allow me to repent and answer the call.

When my co-worker would talk about her wrongdoings but was never willing to make a change, I understood what she was dealing with. She knew what she needed to do, but because of her disobedience towards God, her heart would not allow it. The Bible tells us that when we hear His voice, we should obey right then with no delay. Look at Hebrews:

> For we are made partakers of Christ, if we hold the beginning of our confidence stedfast unto the end; While it is said, Today if ye will hear his voice, harden not your hearts, as in the provocation. For some, when they had heard, did provoke: howbeit not all that came out of Egypt by Moses (Hebrews 3:14-16).

When obedience toward the voice of God or the Word of God is put off for a more convenient time, we are hardening our hearts. It's not God who causes our hearts to harden, but us. We saw the self-inflicted consequences of Jonah's and Pharaoh's disobedience when they were instructed by God to do a certain thing and they refused or procrastinated.

Likewise, the same thing will happen to us when we reject His voice or His Word.

Chapter IV
God Should Have Confidence in Our Obedience

> I write to you [perfectly] confident of your obedient compliance, [a]since I know that you will do even more than I ask (Philemon 21, Amplified Bible).

In the above Scripture, the Apostle Paul was expressing his confidence in Philemon that he would do right by Onesimus, Philemon's runaway slave, by receiving him back. Paul, who was responsible for Philemon's conversion, had so much confidence in Philemon's obedience that he was confident he would not only do what he had asked, but would also do much more. The Bible instructs us on how to live. We should make every effort to follow those instructions. God should have such confidence in us to be obedient to His Word, that when we read something in the Bible that we don't understand, we do our best to comply with what it is telling us to do regardless.

We are told not to shape our way of living based on the world's view, but to convert to the way God says we should live by renewing our minds with the Word of God (Romans 12:2). Renewing our mind gives us the opportunity to focus our thoughts and love on the things that God wants from us instead of the earthly things that are set before us (Colossians 3:2). This is Obedience 101. The goal of every Christian should be to keep their mind renewed to the things of God.

Nothing pleases God more than being able to have confidence that His children will be obedient to Him and His word. Just as an earthly father delights in his children's obedience, likewise, our Heavenly Father takes pleasure knowing that He has confidence in our obedience towards Him. Confidence goes both ways. Scripture tells us that if we have confidence in God, then we can ask anything of Him (that conforms to His Word), He hears us, and we have it (1 John 5:14-15). As we walk with the confidence that God will hear us when we call out to Him, God also desires to have the confidence in us that we will obey Him when He tells us to do something.

There are rewards attached to our confidence in God (Hebrews 10:35). Likewise, when we obey God, He has the confidence that we love Him and have faith in Him. The Bible tells us that there is no way we can please God without faith (Hebrews 11:6).

When Our Obedience is Tested

We believe that God's Word is a test to the believer. Not only to the believer, but to the non-believer also. Both the Old and New Testaments are God's instructions on how man is to live. The words contained within them become tests of our obedience to God. When believers read what God has said, it's now up to them to believe what they read and do what it tells them to do. This is where the test comes into play. It is a test for believers because they simply want to obey God, but cannot bring themselves to it at the time.

When we are tested, especially in our obedience, it can be very challenging on our part. Why? Because most of the time we want to do it our way, or we have a formula or recipe that we want to use. This tends to make obeying God's Word more of a test. Martin Luther King, Jr. said, "The ultimate measure of a man is not where he stands in moments of comfort and convenience, but where he stands at times of challenge and controversy."

We probably won't be tested like Job was, but he is a good example of how we as Christians should respond when we are challenged in obeying God's Word. In Job 22, Job was facing a barrage of criticism from his friends. Despite all the negative words and comments they said, he would not confess, submit, bow down, or obey anything of their words. This was a test for Job. He was being tested on whether he was going to obey God or submit to what his friends were saying.

Even though Job admitted that he didn't know where to find God (Job 23:8-9), he was confident that God knew his heart and would vindicate him. In the midst of his testing, he made this statement:

> Behold, I go forward, but he is not there; and backward, but I cannot perceive him: On the left hand, where he doth work, but I cannot behold him: he hideth himself on the right hand, that I cannot see him: But he knoweth the way that I take: when he hath tried me, I shall come forth as gold. My foot hath held his steps, his way have I kept, and not declined. Neither have I gone back from the commandment of his lips; I have esteemed the words of his mouth more than my necessary food (Job 23:8-12).

This would be hard for most Christians to say, especially after receiving treatment like Job. The point of the whole story is this: Even when we are being tested and it seems like God is far from us, or we feel He doesn't hear us, He still requires our obedience to do what His Word says for us to do. When we are being tested, it can be confusing to make sense of what is going on. All our questions won't be answered, and many times, we are hit with more tests. This is when our obedience to God's Word become crucial in getting through our tests.

James: I want to tell you a true story of something that happened to me while Brenda and I were on vacation. I believe my obedience was put to the test. A few months ago, we were visiting a resort in another state. That night, we were waiting for the shuttle to arrive that would take us back to our hotel. As the shuttle approached the stop, I could see that no other people were on it. The driver stopped, opened the door, and we walked onto the shuttle. We greeted the driver, took a seat close to the front, and she greeted us back with a smile and a hello.

I thought it was kind of strange that we were the only two on the shuttle. At some point, we started to exchange small talk. I felt in my spirit that I should ask her about her salvation status. The first question I asked her was, "Do you attend church?" She replied with confidence, "Yes," and told us the name of the church. Then I said to her, "So, you are a Christian." She again replied with confidence, "Yes," but then she said something relating to how sure she was about her relationship with God.

It went silent for a few seconds. Then, just as I was ready to ask her another question about her salvation, I got a check in my spirit to stop what I was about to say. Because I was tuned in with the Spirit of God, I knew where this check was coming from. One could have seen this check as a hindrance from Satan. After all, it would make sense that it came from the devil, because the devil never wants us to talk to someone about their salvation.

As I sat there submitting myself to the check of my spirit, I anticipated what would come next. During this wait, my eyes were fixed on the mirror where I could see the bus driver's face as she drove down the road. Then, it happened. She looked up and our eyes connected with each other. She said, "Will you pray for my dad?" Her dad needed open heart surgery, and there were some complications around him having the surgery. I prayed for her dad and for her also while she and Brenda agreed. As soon as I was done praying, we arrived at our stop.

We didn't know this lady, neither did she know us. But I have no doubt that this was a God-arranged event. I could have easily spoiled the plan of God by not obeying the check in my spirit. What I was doing by asking her about her salvation was a spiritual thing. God's will that night was for me to stop in the middle of my questioning and allow her to ask for prayer. It took obedience on my part as well as hers.

We will probably never see this lady again on this side of the earth, but I have no doubt that her prayer was answered that night. I believe her dad received the surgery, had a full recovery, and that she had a safe trip to Alabama. I was tested in my obedience to allow God to set up what He wanted to accomplish.

Henrietta Mears said this: "Will is the whole man active. I cannot give up my will; I must exercise it. I must will to obey. When God gives a command or a vision of truth, it is never a question of what He will do, but what we will do. To be successful in God's work is to fall in line with His will and to do it His way. All that is pleasing to Him is a success."

God gives all of us free *will.* We can either exercise our *will* to obey God or exercise our *will to* disobey God. He will allow you to do it either way. Just think, if I had chosen to exercise my *will* that night and continued with my questioning of salvation, then we both would have lost out on the blessings of God. We must be obedient in doing things God's way. When we are obedient to God's *will*, we experience success.

Submission to God is Required When We are Tested

When we are tested in right versus wrong and evil versus good, we must choose to submit to God before we are able to make the right choice. Look at James:

> Submit yourselves therefore to God. Resist the devil, and he will flee from you (James 4:7).

When I hear this verse quoted, it is usually like this: "Resist the devil, and he will flee from you." To be honest, I have quoted it this way before myself. That sounds good, but that is not what the whole verse says. If we *hear* this verse, in this way, it will not work in getting rid of the devil. We are warned about how we *hear* the Word of God, which we will later discuss more in detail.

Notice what it says you must do first: Submit yourself to God. Remember, the word "submit" is the same word as "obey," which according to the American Dictionary of The English Language means: to comply with the commands, orders, or instructions of a superior, or with the requirements of law, moral, political, or municipal; to do that which is commanded or required, or to forbear doing that which is prohibited." The point is that we are to comply with and obey what God has commanded and instructed us to do, and refrain from doing anything that does not submit ourselves to God's Word. Obeying God and what He has said is the first step in getting rid of the devil. There is a process that we must use when we approach this verse for help in getting rid of the devil. You must first obey God, and then resist the devil. That is the order, and the only way that the devil will leave us alone. The devil is not going anywhere if we don't obey God's Word.

Saul (Paul) was Tested by Jesus

We shared with you earlier about when both of us were serving on active duty in the military and how when we were given a command to do something, it was in our best interest to obey. We also said that the Bible is a book filled with commandments from God. All these commandments are directed to the person who chooses to follow Jesus. But here, we want to bring attention to the fact that all obedience and disobedience are proceeded by a command. There must be a command to do something before you can obey or disobey.

In Acts 9, we find the story about how Saul, before his name was changed to Paul, was introduced to Jesus Christ. Saul was on a mission to persecute the church of Jesus Christ and kill those who stood in his way. I am sure Saul was hearing about Jesus and what the Christians were doing throughout the land and vowed to put a stop to it, so he set out to destroy the Christians any way that he could. Look at Acts:

> And desired of him letters to Damascus to the synagogues, that if he found any of this way, whether they were men or women, he might bring them bound unto Jerusalem. And as he journeyed, he came near Damascus: and suddenly there shined round about him a light from heaven: And he fell to the earth, and heard a voice saying unto him, Saul, Saul, why persecutest thou me? And he said, Who art thou, Lord? And the Lord said, I am Jesus whom thou persecutest: it is hard for thee to kick against the pricks. And he trembling and astonished said, Lord, what wilt thou have me to do? And the Lord said unto him, Arise, and go into the city, and it shall be told thee what thou must do (Acts 9:2-6).

This is the revelation we want you to get: Jesus commanded Saul to do something. He told Saul, "Arise and go into the city." Saul was given a command by Jesus, and he had the choice to obey or disobey. Saul could have ignored the command of Jesus and chose to continue in his old ways. We believe that if Saul had chosen to disobey, then his name wouldn't have been changed to Paul, we wouldn't be reading about him, and he wouldn't have written over half of the New Testament. It is no different for any other person. We all have the choice to exercise our *free will* by either obeying the Word of God or disobeying the Word of God.

Let's look at another example of Jesus giving a command that required a response of obedience or disobedience. This story is found in three of the gospel books, but we will look at it from Mark:

> And he entered again into the synagogue; and there was a man there which had a withered hand. And they watched him, whether he would heal him on the sabbath day; that they might accuse him. And he saith unto the man which had the withered hand, Stand forth. And he saith unto them, Is it lawful to do good on the sabbath days, or to do evil? to save life, or to kill? But they held their peace. And when he had looked round about on them with anger, being grieved for the hardness of their hearts, he saith unto the man, Stretch forth thine hand. And he stretched it out: and his hand was restored whole as the other (Mark 3:1-5).

Here we see Jesus doing what only He can do—healing the sick. In this story, we see Jesus giving two commands to the person needing healing. It's important to point out that the people observing Jesus' actions were not there to support Him, but rather to find fault in Him.

But Jesus made it crystal clear that His intention was to heal the man. Jesus did this by first commanding the man to stand, so that all His critics could see what He was about to do. Notice, the man was given the command, "Stand forth." The man had a choice to obey Jesus' command or disobey it. The text does not say that the man stood up as Jesus commanded, but it is implied he did, because Jesus began to address His critics concerning the man. After Jesus was finished calling out His faultfinders, He commanded the man to stretch forth his hand, which the man obeyed.

This man was healed of a withered hand because he decided to obey the commands of Jesus. These were two simple commands, "Stand forth," and "Stretch forth thine hand." It took very little physical effort on the man's part to comply or obey the commands of Jesus. A command will always be preparatory to obedience or disobedience.

In the book of 1 Kings, we read the story about the prophet Elijah being commanded by God to go to Zarephath, and dwell there, because God had commanded a widow woman to care for him. Look at 1 Kings:

> So he arose and went to Zarephath. And when he came to the gate of the city, behold, the widow woman was there gathering of sticks: and he called to her, and said, Fetch me, I pray thee, a little water in a vessel, that I may drink. And as she was going to fetch it, he called to her, and said, Bring me, I pray thee, a morsel of bread in thine hand. And she said, As the Lord thy God liveth, I have not a cake, but an handful of meal in a barrel, and a little oil in a cruse: and, behold, I am gathering two sticks, that I may go in and dress it for me and my son, that we may eat it, and die. And Elijah said unto her, Fear not; go and do as thou hast said: but make me thereof a little cake first, and bring it unto me, and after make for thee and for thy son. For thus saith the Lord God of Israel, The barrel of meal shall not waste, neither shall the cruse of oil fail, until the day that the

Lord sendeth rain upon the earth. And she went and did according to the saying of Elijah: and she, and he, and her house, did eat many days. And the barrel of meal wasted not, neither did the cruse of oil fail, according to the word of the Lord, which he spake by Elijah (1 Kings 17:10-16).

Every time this story is told, it reminds us of how God can test us with the material things in our lives. God used something so important as food to get His blessing to this woman. You might be saying, "How can this be true?" Our answer is "Because it's in the Bible." It may be hard for some to believe that a widow would give her last food to a total stranger when she has kept it for her and her son as a last meal before they die. But what we want you to see is how her obedience led to her blessings. This widow was tested by God. She could have easily said, "No! This is all the food we have, and it's only enough for me and my son." Any excuse she gave would have been justified, but her obedience to do what the prophet Elijiah commanded caused the oil and meal to multiply for many days. We could say that she passed that obedience test.

Another lesson we can take from that story is this: Whatever we have, no matter how important it is to us and to God, He has a way of getting more to us. We just need to trust Him and obey Him.

Once again, we will look back at our time in the military. In drills and ceremonies, there is a preparatory command followed by an execution command. You are commanded to perform a certain movement, followed up with a command to carry out the movement.

Let us give you an example. When a leader wants to get the attention of a squad, platoon, battalion, or any group of soldiers, he calls them to attention. The word "attention" simply means to be attentive and give ear to the person giving the command. When the word "attention" is given, it is given in a two-part command. The first part, "atten-" is the preparatory command, which tells the person hearing the command to prepare for a follow-up command. The second part, "-tion" is the execution command, which tells the person to complete the drill movement.

This example is a good illustration of how we come to obey or disobey. In all our lives, we are given a preparatory command, and then we have the choice of executing that command by obedience or disobedience. In the story above, Jesus gave the preparatory commands, "Stand" and "Stretch forth," followed by the execution commands, "Forth" and "Thine hand."

The bottom line of the story is this: commands require us to obey or disobey. It comes down to compliance or non-compliance, submitting or resisting.

Obedience Requires a Renewed Mind

Many times, our minds are consumed with issues that we are faced with in life, such as worry, anxiety, stress, disappointment, failure, and lack. We know these things don't come from God, but somehow, they have the tendency to weigh us down. Therefore, we focus more on them than we focus on what God has said. This redirected focus causes us to disobey what God has said and focus instead on what we know or feel.

Satan loves to play mind games with people. But we as Christians have been given a defense against his games. Before we can submit to God's Word, we must first understand what God's Word says. It's called the renewing of the mind. Look at Romans:

> And be not conformed to this world: but be ye transformed by the renewing of your mind, that ye may prove what is that good, and acceptable, and perfect, will of God (Romans 12:2).

We could say that our good, acceptable, and perfect will towards God is when we submit ourselves and be obedient to Him and His Word. When we decide to submit ourselves to God's way of doing things, we totally agree to push back on what the world has to offer. When we renew our mind and transform our mind to the Word of God, obedience is the by-product. Where there is no renewing of the mind, there is no transformation. Where there is no transformation, there is no obedience.

We want you to notice something from the verse above. When our minds are renewed and transformed, it's not our doing. It's God. But the only way God can do this is by our total surrender to Him. He must have all of us to renew and transform our minds the way Paul describes. This is why it is almost impossible for some people to obey God.

Chapter V
Disobedience Leads to Deception

Brenda: I have been challenged many times in my walk with God to obey Him. I remember a time when I decided to do things my way and disregard what God told me to do. When we first moved to Knoxville after my husband had served a tour in Okinawa, Japan, I started to look for a job. I believed the Lord had told me to apply for a certain job and instructed me on what I was to do. I obtained all the paperwork necessary to apply for the job. It was a lot of paperwork to fill out, and I didn't want to do it. After a few days of fumbling through them, I took all those papers and laid them on the kitchen table, and I never went back to them.

Days later, I found myself seeking another position at a different employer. Well, I can tell you that decision didn't at all work out well for me. I allowed Satan to get into my ear by avoiding the original paperwork and seeking a different position. I had walked away from what God had told me to do and chose what I wanted to do instead.

I had no problem getting the job that I had chosen. Some of you might be saying, "Well, that must have been the job God wanted you to have." No. It was not the job God had planned for me. One thing about God is that He will allow us to have free will over our life and the decisions we make.

What I was really telling God was that the job that I had chosen was better for me than the one He had chosen. Thank God for His grace and mercy. I was working on this job for a little over a month. I began to sense that I had made a bad move. I told God that was the hardest job I had ever performed. God firmly answered me and said, "That's not what I told you to do. That's what you wanted to do." At that moment, I knew I had not obeyed. But to be honest, I knew I was not being obedient from the beginning.

That next week, I collected all those papers I had laid on the kitchen table and filled them out. I delivered them, and in just a few days, I was hired for that position. God will let us do what we want to do. He doesn't force Himself on you. While obedience leads to blessing, disobedience leads to deception. The devil didn't want me to be in God's will.

I remember when I first joined the military. I had to comply with and obey the commands that were given to me. Whatever I was told to do, and how I was told to do it, I was expected to do. I recall one day when everyone in the formation was ordered to double time, which means run, I decided I was going to walk. I quickly found out that my disobedience would cost me some pushups. My disobedience led me to believe that I could walk while everyone else ran, and there wouldn't be any consequences. I was deceived by my own way of thinking That was a long time ago, but disobedience to God will always have a price tag attached to it. Most of the time, it's a price we don't want to pay.

Brenda's story reminds us of a question that comes to mind quite often: What if Adam obeyed God in the garden? What would the world be like if Adam and Eve didn't fall for the devil's deception? Because of their disobedience, sin entered the world, they were evicted from the garden, women would have pain during childbirth, man would have to work for food, and a list of other problems were created (Genesis 3). The consequences of their actions are haunting mankind centuries after that day. Because of one's man disobedience, we have to live in a world of sin (Romans 5:12).

Just like Saul and Moses, Adam had clear and concise instructions from God Himself about what trees to eat from and what tree not to eat from. But because of the deceptive and crafty speech of the devil, Adam and Eve disobeyed God.

God will not wait a long time for us to obey Him. He will quietly move on to someone else to perform His *will* on the earth. When He tells us to do something, whether it's by the leading of His Holy Spirit, or by speaking to us through His Word, we are to not procrastinate. We are not saying that you should be gullible to everything you hear, because we know there are many voices (1 Corinthians 14:10). But what we must remember is that all the voices that come to us do have meaning. Some just have the wrong meaning. Jesus said that His sheep hear His voice, know His voice, and don't listen to any other (John 10:27). So, we obey when we hear the voice of God, because we know the voice of God, and we reject any other voice.

Disobedience brings deception, and we cannot operate in the realm of deception if we want to receive God's blessings. Disobedience separates believers from God.

 Bulkeley is correct. If we love God like we say we do and put our faith in Him like we claim we do, then we must be obedient to His Word and to the leading of the Holy Spirit.

Loving Jesus is the Prerequisite to Obeying Him

In our King James Bible, there are certain words or chapters that are printed in red. We know that these are the words of Jesus, the Head of the Church. When Jesus tells us to do something, to live a certain way, talk a certain way, or to do a certain thing, then I think we ought to obey Him.

Earlier we said that the word "obedient" also means "Hupakouo" in the Hebrew, which means: to listen attentively; or to heed or conform to a command or authority. I want to look at the word "command" a little deeper. Let's look at the word "command" from Jesus' perspective. Jesus commanded us to do a lot of things. Look at John:

> If ye love me, keep my commandments
> (John 14:15).

This is a short verse, but it is packed with a lot of truth. It says a lot about whether we obey Jesus or not. You could read the above verse as: "If we love Jesus, we will obey and do what He has told us to do." To love Jesus is to obey Him. It's just that simple. Obedience to Jesus and His Word is the master key to unlocking the blessing of God in our lives. God requires 100% obedience from us. We have seen through Moses and Jonah that anything less is not acceptable to God.

There is a lot more we could say about love. The word "love" is an important word coming out of the mouth of Jesus. We believe that our salvation stems from love. John 3:16, a verse which most people are familiar with, tells us that God loved the world so much that He gave His only Son, Jesus, to die for its sins. The Bible also tells us that love covers a lot of the sins that we commit (1 Peter 4:8). Think about that for a minute. When we disobey Jesus by not following His commandments, we therefore don't love Him. And because we don't love Him, we sin. Jesus has already covered our sins with His love. All we must do is submit to and obey His commandments.

Jesus even told us to love our enemy (Matthew 5:44). You might be saying, "What was He thinking—love our enemy? He doesn't know the people I have to deal with." Jesus knows exactly who our enemies are. As a matter of fact, He probably sent some of them our way just to see how we would react. Obeying Jesus' commands could be a lot easier for us if we would only commit to loving Jesus with all our heart, soul, mind, and strength (Mark 12:30). To love Jesus and God this way takes everything we have. But if it wasn't possible, He would not have instructed us to do it.

Jesus didn't stop there. He commanded us to love our neighbors as we love ourselves (Mark 12:31). Some of us know how hard this can be at times. But Jesus would not have told us to do it if we could not. It's the love for Him that gives us the power to love others, even an unlovable neighbor. Our job is not to examine others to see if they are qualified to be loved. Our job is to love and obey. Let's look at John:

> Judas, not Iscariot, asked Him, Lord, how is it that You will reveal Yourself [make Yourself real] to us and not to the world? Jesus answered, If a person [really] loves Me, he will keep My word [obey My teaching]; and My Father will love him, and We will come to him and make Our home

(abode, special dwelling place) with him (John 14:22-23, Amplified Bible, Classic Edition).

Our obedience towards Jesus originates from our love for Him. There is no other way to put it. The translation above uses the phrase, "really loves Me." We all know what the word "really" means. Jesus is saying, *"If you are really telling the truth about loving me, then you will have no problem obeying and keeping My Word."* Our love for Jesus will be shown by how we respond to what He has told us to do and what the Holy Spirit prompts us to do. Loving Jesus will always be the true challenge to passing the test of obedience. Look at John again:

> Those who do not love me do not ·obey my teaching [L keep my words]. This ·teaching [word] that you hear is not really mine; it is from my Father, who sent me (John 14:24, Expanded Bible).

Scripture states that we can tell who a person is by the fruit that they bear (Matthew 7:20). We know this verse refers to identifying false prophets, but we think it could apply to any behavior. It can apply to our obedience toward Jesus. In the same way a false prophet is known by the fruit they bear, likewise, an obedient Christian is known by their love for Jesus. Jesus could not have said it any plainer. If there is not love for Jesus, there is no obeying Him.

Brenda: I was recently challenged to obey God when we decided to raise money to purchase a wheelchair van for my elderly sister. She desperately needed a van to transport her back and forth to doctors' appointments, and so that she could attend church. After several days of the process, I felt that things were not going as quickly as I thought they should or wanted them to. I was praying and asking God to lead us to the perfect wheelchair mobility van for my disabled sister. As my husband, James, was searching and making phone calls, I was praying.

Amid the fundraising, the Lord spoke to me and instructed me to give a substantially large amount towards the purchase of the van. I first hesitated and started to make excuses about why I couldn't do that. When the Lord tells us to do something, He is not wondering whether we are capable, because He knows we are. This is something that every Christian must understand. God will not instruct us to do something that He hasn't prepared us to do. The question is, are we willing to obey Him? In one of our bedrooms, we have a plaque hanging on the wall that reads: "The *will* of God will never take you, where the grace of God will not protect you." I knew it was God's *will* for me to give the money, because He would never have told me to give it if I didn't have it to give.

So, after a few nudges from the Holy Spirit, I obeyed and gave the amount I was *hearing*. The next day or two later, I was told to give again and the amount. This did not happen once or twice, but three different times. I did what God instructed me to do. I am thankful I obeyed God's commands. The very first time He told me to give, I didn't receive it as a suggestion, but as a command. It was an authoritative order from the Person I put my trust in, and I know that He is my Supplier. The Bible says, "Always remember that it is the Lord your God who gives you power to become rich, and he does it to fulfill his promise to your ancestors" (Deuteronomy 8:18, Living Bible). I wanted to use this translation, because I think it puts emphasis on that we should *always* remember so that we do not forget.

After we had met our fundraising goal, people continued to give. James was able to find the perfect wheelchair van for my sister. It was what we had been praying for. I know that some people might say, "It probably would have happened anyway if you hadn't given those large amounts you were told to give." I have no doubt that it would have happened. But to me, being obedient to God's instructions was more important than the money or worrying about what the next person was giving. I asked God for something, and He in return told me to do something. It all goes back to having faith in God and loving Him. We know that faith without work won't achieve anything good (James 2:20).

We can say how much we love God, His Word, Jesus, the Holy Spirit, and people, but if we fail to obey what the Word of God says, there is no proof of love for Him. We are simply quoting what we have read from the Bible, which is good, but we are not to be only hearers of the Word, but also doers of the Word (James 1:22). James goes on to tell us in that verse that when we hear and fail to do, it causes a deception in our lives. When we fail to do what Jesus has told us to do, we are disobeying Him and deceiving ourselves. This disobedience causes us to live with deceit in our heart.

Jesus is saying that our obedience toward Him is the real test to keeping His commandments. Our love for Jesus is a choice of our *will*. To truly love Jesus is a *willingness* to keep His commandments. Our obedience to Jesus will always be driven by our love for Him.

I have no doubt that my willingness to obey when I was instructed to give those large amounts of money was directly connected to receiving exactly what I was praying for in a wheelchair van. In my walk as a Christian, I have learned that being obedience is completely my choice. It's an act of my faith and my own *will.* And it's like that for all of us. God, Jesus, or the Holy Spirit, will make us do nothing outside of our will. Whatever we do or become in life is based on the choices we make. God allows everyone the freedom to choose.

Chapter VI
Our Blessings are a Result of Our Obedience

The only way we can keep Jesus' commandments is that each of us have a personal relationship with Him. When we seek him when making decisions, we are honoring Him through our obedience to Him. Because we love Him, we aim to please Him, which is done through our obedience to His commandments. Just like a husband or wife would do whatever they could to please their spouse, likewise, we are to please Jesus by being obedience to keep His commandments.

We have already said this, but a "command" is not a suggestion. It's a requirement. If we expect to receive God's blessings, then it is required of us to obey His commandments. The Bible teaches us that Jesus Christ learned obedience through the things He suffered. Look at Hebrews:

> While Jesus lived on earth he prayed to God, asking for help from the one who could save him from death. He prayed to God with loud cries and tears. And his prayers were answered because of his great respect for God. Jesus was the Son of God, but he still suffered, and through his sufferings he learned to obey whatever God says. This made him the perfect high priest, who provides the way for everyone who obeys him to be saved forever (Hebrews 7:9, Easy-to-Read Version).

These verses tell us that our Lord and Savior, Jesus Christ, had to experience some hardship before He obeyed the Father. Sometimes, it's no different for us as His children. Many times, we must go through hardship, lack, discomfort, and other afflictions before we come to our senses and obey God. But this is never the way God desires for us to live life. Jesus' sufferings were for the world's salvation (John 3:16). When we suffer, it is because of our own disobedience or the disobedience of someone else. But they both are directly related to sin. Look at Romans:

> And not as it was by one that sinned, so is the gift: for the judgment was by one to condemnation, but the free gift is of many offences unto justification. For if by one man's offence death reigned by one; much more they which receive abundance of grace and of the gift of righteousness shall reign in life by one, Jesus Christ. Therefore as by the offence of one judgment came upon all men to condemnation; even so by the righteousness of one the free gift came upon all men unto justification of life (Romans 16:18).

Earlier, we discussed Adam's disobedience, but we want to point out that all sin can be contributed to him. There is a major contrast in those verses between one who obeyed God and one who disobeyed God. Adam's disobedience brought about judgment, resulting in disapproval from God. But Jesus' obedience brought about justification (Romans 5:16).

Jesus' obedience took precedence over Adam's disobedience. This is important for us to know. When we obey God, we can expect His blessings. But when we disobey Him, we can expect a curse. It is not God who is cursing us, but rather the curse comes as a result of our disobedience. We see this throughout the entire 28 chapters of Deuteronomy.

Because of Jesus' obedience, the whole world was blessed. Because of Adam's disobedience, the world was cursed. Jesus' obedience was a sacrificial obedience. He sacrificed His own life for the life of every person that would be born into the world, just as Abraham was willing to sacrifice his son, Isaac (Genesis 22:1-18). But look what verse 18 says:

> And in thy seed shall all the nations of the earth be blessed; because thou hast obeyed my voice (Genesis 22:18).

God provided a lamb for Abraham's offerings for Him. We are the seed of Abraham. Because of Abraham's willingness to obey God, we are blessed. When we obey God, He will provide for us whatever we need. That's what the words "Jehovah Jireh" mean. The Lord is our Provider and will provide for us (Genesis 22:14). Jesus is our sacrificial Lamb who was slain before the foundation of the world (Revelation 13:8).

There is an event recorded in the Bible about obedience that we want to share with you. Notice, this is not a parable that Jesus used to make His point with His disciples, but an actual event. Look at Luke:

> Now when he had left speaking, he said unto Simon, Launch out into the deep, and let down your nets for a draught. And Simon answering said unto him, Master, we have

toiled all the night, and have taken nothing: nevertheless at thy word I will let down the net. And when they had this done, they inclosed a great multitude of fishes: and their net brake (Luke 5:4-6).

This story is a great example of how we are blessed when we are obedient to what Jesus tells us to dot. Peter could have missed out on his blessing if he chose to disobey Jesus' command for him to launch out into the deep and let down his nets. Because of Peter's obedience, he and his fishing partners caught more fish at the command of Jesus than they would have probably caught in a whole week. Our obedience has a way of turning our disappointments and shortcomings into successes and blessings.

Another example of a person receiving his blessing because of his obedience to Jesus' command can be found in the book of John. In chapter nine we find the story of a man born blind. After Jesus was finished educating His disciples on why the man was born blind, He began to deal with the blind man. Let's look a little closer at the Scripture:

When he had thus spoken, he spat on the ground, and made clay of the spittle, and he anointed the eyes of the blind man with the clay, And said unto him, Go, wash in the pool of Siloam, (which is by interpretation, Sent.) He went his way therefore, and washed, and came seeing (John 9:6-7).

Jesus could have supernaturally caused the man to see, but He chose otherwise. Jesus evidently wanted the man to use his faith and obey what he was told to do. Jesus performed an act. He spat on the ground, made clay of the spittle, and anointed the blind man's eyes with the clay, and then gave the man a command: go and wash in the pool of Siloam.

This man's healing required an act of his faith and obedience. Jesus commanded the man to do something, and the man obeyed and did it. When the man obeyed and washed his face in the pool, he received his sight and could see for the first time in his life. This man was blessed with his sight all because of his faith and obedience to act on what Jesus told him to do. The blessings in our lives are directly related to our obedience to do what God tells us to do. When we don't obey, we bring a curse on ourselves and prevent the blessings of God upon our lives.

When We Disobey, We Sin

Now, back to the wheelchair van experience. We both were being instructed by God to do our part in procuring the van. I sort of relate this to where the Bible talks about the body having many members, but they all have different tasks (Romans 12:4). Each of us had different duties to complete to possess the van.

James: While Brenda's duties were to pray and give money, my duties were to pray and look or locate. The Lord said to me, "There are some things that men are better at doing." That is not in any way a putdown to women or meant to degrade women. When the Lord spoke those words to me, they were for that specific purpose, for that task. The Lord was telling me that in that scenario, I was more knowledgeable in dealing with the process of looking for and selecting the wheelchair van.

All men were created to be leaders. Granted, we are not all gifted in the same area. We all have our weaknesses and strengths. Some are more gifted at one thing, while some are more gifted at others. That's just the way God wired us. But even our individual gifts sometimes require development. When we as men see a need, especially in our own family, we ought to step up to the plate as leaders and help to fulfill that need. I am not talking about taking control or running over people. But, if you have strengths in that area and you sit back and allow a problem to grow bigger or become a burden, you are not doing what God anointed you to do as a leader. And that is disobedience.

You might say, "But God didn't tell me to get involved." Maybe He didn't speak directly to you, but He has already given you everything needed to do the job. We just must be obedient, get involved, and allow Him to bring out the gift in us. Again, I am not suggesting being controlling or pushy, but you should at least offer your assistance, especially if God has gifted and anointed you in a certain area. If your help isn't welcomed, I am sure you will be told.

However, if someone asks for your assistance and you agree to help, there may come a time when you might have to go it alone. Looking for a wheelchair van for my sister-in-law turned out to be one of those times. I was asked to help in finding a wheelchair van. I won't say that I was tasked with the responsibility, but rather that I took on the responsibility. I took on the responsibility because I saw there was a need, and I knew I was gifted and anointed in this area.

So, we went to work raising money. As I witnessed Brenda's desire to get her sister a wheelchair van and how God was dealing with her about giving, I knew I had to be obedient and do my part. I watched how she was being obedient to give every time she was led to give. I began searching for a wheelchair van. We finally raised enough money where we thought we could get a good used wheelchair van.

The Lord had given me a plan to quickly get a van, and I began to put that plan into action. I was well into working that plan. I continued to look for vans on the internet, searching every website I knew. I was being obedient and doing what the Lord had instructed me to do.

After a few weeks, I realized that I were being offered help with the details of the plan that God had given me. I saw the plan that God had given me slowly turn into a struggle. I knew in my heart that this was not the way God had instructed me to this. I begin to feel a little discouraged and frustrated. I knew I had steered away from God's plan.

While I was praying one morning, I heard the Lord say these words to me, "There are some things that men are better at doing." At first, I didn't know what to think or how to process what I had heard. I ignored that warning from the Lord and proceeded with the way others were telling me. I say it was a warning because He knew where this whole thing was headed if I didn't change directions to do it the way He had instructed. I knew what Brenda was praying for, and there were no questions about what God had told me to do. I recognized the anointing on me for this. There was no doubt in my mind about what I was to do. I knew what to look for, the questions to ask, and where to seek help. I understood my role in this project, and it was my responsibility to see it through.

Another week passed, and we still didn't have a van. It seemed that the process was getting more and more difficult every day and I was feeling more and more defeated with each passing day. Of course, I kept all this to myself. The problem wasn't that I couldn't locate a van. I found plenty of vans. The problem was that I allowed other people, good people, who meant no harm, to speak into the situation and alter the direction the Lord had instructed me to go in. This was not what God had planned, but I allowed it to happen because I didn't want to hurt other people's feelings. I realized that I must put a stop to this. So, I got before the Lord and repented.

I told the Lord that if He gave me another chance to make this right, that I would do it the way He initially instructed me to do. God gave me that chance. This Scripture came to mind:

> The sorrow that God uses makes people sorry for their sin and leads them to turn from sin so they can be saved from the punishment of sin. We should be happy for that kind of sorrow, but the sorrow of this world brings death (2 Corinthians 7:10, New Life Version).

I know that the above Scripture deals with salvation of the soul. But I believe that God can use sorrow and frustration in our life to cause us to change for the better in many areas. God never wants to see us continue down a road that He knows has a dead end or one where the outcome will not be in our favor. I was truly sorrowful for the way I had handled the task God gave me and knew that repenting was the way to stop the bleeding of self-punishment in my life. What was happening to me was self-inflicted. My disobedience to what the Lord had told me to do was my sin, and I was the only one able to correct it. The Bible tells us that when we know what is right to do and we don't do it, then it's a sin to us (James 4:17).

Someone else might not consider what I did a sin, but I did. And any time we sin, it requires repenting and then doing what we know is right, if we still have the opportunity to do so. Many times, when we sin by not doing what we know to be right, we don't get a second chance to make it right. But whether we have a second chance or not, it still requires repenting for our disobedience.

Sometimes when we are given a second chance, we often think that God will give us new instructions. He could, but that's not always the case. In my situation, a second chance came with the initial instructions God had for obtaining the van. Thank God I was granted the chance to right the wrong of my disobedience.

Other than a lesson in obedience, I learned that when God is doing something new, don't try to take what was old and lump it into the new. Let me explain. After God granted me a second chance, some of the same people that I allowed to cloud my judgment before were attempting to do it again. All the advice and comments started all over again. They were telling me how they thought it should be done, or if it were them, they would do this or do that. The reason things didn't go as planned the first time was because I failed to follow the plan that was given to me by God. I know these people meant well and were just trying to help. I think there are times in our lives where we all try to help God out. Newsflash! God doesn't need our help doing anything.

So, now that God had given me a second chance, I was not about to allow what was done and said the first time to be brought into the new opportunity that God had given me. It was a chance to make my wrong, right. God didn't give me any new instructions the second time that He hadn't given me the first time. No new instructions, just a new opportunity. It wasn't that God's plan had failed. Rather, I failed to properly execute God's plan. I didn't have a new or different task or goal. The task or goal was the same as before—to acquire a good wheelchair van. That didn't change. God didn't give me a new or different plan; He just granted me a new beginning to His original plan. The same way He had instructed me from the beginning is the same way He was instructing me to do it the second time around.

This time, I had to do it on my own, other than with the help of God, of course. Also, because I value Brenda's advice and suggestions, I continued to seek her input and did my best to keep her informed of what was going on. Every time I located a wheelchair van, I would show her pictures and tell her details about it. However, I didn't allow her comments and suggestions to sway what the Lord had told me. When I disobeyed God the first time, I lost vision after several failed attempts to procure a van. But after being granted a second chance, I gained a new vision, a new perspective, a new focus, and could not allow the old, what was, to become part of the new opportunity God had given me.

I know I was anointed and appointed to make this happen. I had seen what happened before and the results I got. So, now that God had granted me with a new chance, I was not going to allow the old ways that were used before to attempt to procure a van, to be lumped into the new opportunity I was granted. To do this would have been insanity on my part. Again, the plan was the same, but God gave me an opportunity for a new chance. This was my opportunity to prove to God that my desire is to obey Him instead of obeying man (Acts 5:29). I said earlier that I did what I did because I didn't want to hurt anyone's feelings, but I knew that neither my feelings nor the feelings of others compared to pleasing God. I knew better, I just failed at doing better. My mother uses to say, "When you know better, you should do better."

The Bible has something to say about mixing old things with new things. In Matthew 9:17, Jesus said, "Neither do men put new wine into old bottles: else the bottles break, and the wine runneth out, and the bottles perish: but they put new wine into new bottles, and both are preserved."

The verse above is in reference to the new life that Jesus brings. When we are born again, our old way of living is over and done with and we begin to live a new way (2 Corinthians 5:17). Jesus is the new wine being placed into a new body with a new way of living. Because we now have a new spirit, the old things that we used to subject our body to will not mix with the new spirit.

Likewise, when God gives us something new, He does not want old ideals, old ways, or old suggestions used to try and bring His plan to pass. If it failed the first time, it is bound to fail the second time.

God and His Word Never Change

God and His Word will never change (Hebrews 13:8; James 1:17). So please don't hear me saying that God changes His

Word when He allowed us a second chance. That is not what I'm saying. In this case, some people were trying to bring their old ideals, that didn't work before, and inject them into the new opportunity God had granted me. When God gives us something, we should always consider it to be new to us. Why would God give me new instruction the second time around? It's not like God made a mistake the first time. God's way is always a *new* way. When we obey God, we can rest assured that the details of His plan are new even if they are for a second chance. Look at Ecclesiastes:

> Words cannot fully explain things,[a] but people continue speaking.[b] Words come again and again to our ears, but our ears don't become full. And our eyes don't become full of what we see. All things continue the way they have been since the beginning. The same things will be done that have always been done. There is nothing new in this life. Someone might say, "Look, this is new," but that thing has always been here. It was here before we were (Ecclesiastes 1:8-10, Easy-to-Read Version).

I like these verses in this translation. Sometimes, we are under the impression that because God gives us a second chance, He changes His original plans for us. We can try to rationalize that just because we have a second chance, things must be new from God's viewpoint. But, from God's viewpoint, the plan is the same—to help me locate a van. What was different is that He gave me a *new* hope, a *new* vision, a *new* drive, and a *new* focus to achieve His original plan. God didn't change, but He changed me. He changed my way of thinking. He changed my attitude. And most of all, He changed the way I submitted myself to Him. God was telling me that His way of having me find a van didn't change just because it didn't work out the first time. He granted me a new opportunity, but His way for me to do it did not change. Many times, we look at a new chance, a new opportunity, and mistakenly think that means a new way or new instructions. God doesn't change His mind because we fail to obey Him (Hebrews 13:8). He also doesn't make mistakes like we do (Deuteronomy 32:4; Psalms 18:30; and Matthew 5:48).

The only way we can know and follow God's plan for our life is by obeying what He tells us to do. John Calvin said, "All true knowledge of God is born out of obedience." No Christian wakes up in the morning with the thought of sinning against God. But what most Christians don't realize is that when they disobey Him, they are sinning against Him and themselves.

I have another true story I want to share with you. I find it so supernatural that I get chills just thinking about it. It is truly a story about obedience and one that Brenda and I will never forget. I won't go into the full details of this supernatural event at this time, but I will share the highlights. If you choose to hear about this story in its entirety, you can read about it in my book, "A God-Balanced Life."

Early one morning, around 1:30 A M we were driving on a dark country road. Our car broke down, and we were stuck on the side of the road with nowhere to go and no way to contact anyone. To make things worse, we were the only car on the road that night.

After trying to start the car several times with no success, we sat inside the car for what seemed like an hour, but was more like fifteen minutes. The entire time we were sitting there, not one car appeared on the road in either direction.

With no traffic at all, no streetlights, and not one house in sight, I called out to Jesus. I said, "Jesus, You have got to send someone." Those were my exact words. Immediately after those words came out of my mouth, I looked in the rearview mirror and saw a light in the far distance. Then I heard these words in my spirit, "That's your ride." I told Brenda I saw what looked like a car light coming and that I was going to flag it down. She looked at me and replied, "You don't know those people." And I replied, "That's our ride. Lock the doors when I get out."

I got out of the car and stood on the side of the road waving my flashlight. As the vehicle got closer, I could see it was a church van. They agreed to give us a ride to the nearest open gas station. I continued to thank the driver for helping us. While we were talking, I learned from the passenger that we were relatives on my grandmother's side. Talking about experiencing the supernatural!

Imagine the Spirit of God is telling you to do something that goes against what your flesh is telling you. It happens to me all the time. Most of us would follow the guidance of the flesh because it seems and feels more natural than what the Spirit is saying. This is why I say it was a supernatural event.

The people in the van were our blessing that night. Had I not obeyed, got out of the car, and flagged them down, I don't know how that morning would have turned out. This was clearly obedience on my part. Yes, I had a choice to follow my flesh, which at the time, felt much better than what the Spirit was telling me. Even though I never heard the words, "Get out of the car and stop the vehicle," I knew those actions are what would bring us the victory that morning. I had to have faith in God, which was expressed by obeying what I heard and putting action with it. To again quote what A.W. Tozer said, "The Bible recognizes no faith that does not lead to obedience, nor does it recognize any obedience that does not spring from faith. The two are at opposite sides of the same coin."

Remember, if we don't believe and have faith, then we cannot submit to or obey what we are being told. It was an act of obedience to God that morning that supernaturally delivered us to safety. My disobedience could have easily led us into a more dangerous situation. Blessing comes with obedience and curses come with disobedience. I am reminded of this verse in Psalms:

> Great blessings belong to those who don't listen to evil advice, who don't live like sinners, and who don't join those who make fun of God. [a] (Psalm 1:1, Easy-to-Read Version).

Evil advice can come in many forms. It can come through our ears, our eyes, and through our feelings. The evil advice I was getting that morning was coming from my flesh. I knew I could not trust my flesh outside of what I was told by the Spirit. I knew that nothing good could come from my flesh (John 6:63). The struggle of obeying the Spirit or obeying our flesh is something we will contend with as long as we live, because the Spirit and the flesh are constantly at odds with each other (Galatians 5:17).

Chapter VII
Be Quick to Obey God

Woe unto them that call evil good, and good
evil; that put darkness for light, and light for
darkness; that put bitter for sweet, and sweet
for bitter! (Isaiah 5:20).

We talked earlier about how disobedience leads to
deception. We are living in a time of great deception. Jesus
Himself, the Head of the Church tells us to be careful not to
allow man to deceive us (Matthew 24:4). The Bible also
states that we can deceive ourselves (1 Corinthians 3:17-19).
According to the Bible, there are many ways that we can
deceive ourselves. But one of the ways we can deceive
ourselves is by disobedience. The devil is a master at
deception. Look at Revelation:

And the great dragon was cast out, that old
serpent, called the Devil, and Satan, which
deceiveth the whole world: he was cast out
into the earth, and his angels were cast out
with him (Revelation 12:9).

Satan's mission is to bring deception upon the
people of God. That's why it's vitally important to
know and understand the commandments of God
and be quick to obey them. Being quick to obey is a
sure-fire way to avoid falling into deception.

Because we don't always get a second chance to obey God,
we should not hesitate when He instructs us to do
something. When we postpone in doing what God has told
us to do, we consider it to be disobedience. We can be

disobedient, as the saying goes, "Until the cows come home." It doesn't matter if we are disobedient for a day, a week, a month, or a year, it's still disobedience, and it will not alter the plan and will of God. Someone might say, "But I did what the Lord told me to do. I just didn't do it when He told me to do it." When God tells us to do something, He didn't mean tomorrow, next week, or next year, He meant do it at the time He told you. Granted, there are times when His instructions are for a later date, but He will make that clear in those cases.

The Bible states that whoever hears the Word of God and does it is blessed (Luke 11:28). This doesn't just mean *hearing* the Word of God from the Bible, but it also means *hearing* when God speaks to us in our spirit. Many times, when reading the words from the Bible, the words that we hear ourselves saying are instructions for a current problem or issue we are experiencing in our life. Once again, we know that we need to act and do what the Word of God is telling us to do, but we hesitate, put off, or dismiss what we are being instructed to do.

Many of the translations for the verse we used above used the word "keep" or "obey." But we want to look at another translation.

> Jesus replied, "But even more blessed are all who hear the word of God and put it into practice (Luke 11:28, New Living Translation).

Here we learn that we are to put the Word of God into practice as we hear it. So, we obey by keeping the Word and by practicing the Word. When Jesus told us to love our neighbors as we love ourselves, He didn't mean to wait until our neighbors are loveable, He meant love them in the moment.

Remember when you were a child and your parents told you to do something? All of us can probably relate to one of those times. But most of the time, because of our childish behavior, we hesitated or delayed in doing what we were told to do. In our household, that did not always work out to our advantage. Often, we had to be told repeatedly. We may not have said it out loud, but we were really thinking was, "I'll do it when I want," or, "They didn't mean right now." Many times, we also wanted our parents to explain why they were telling us to do something.

As we got older, we started to realize that the things our parents were telling us to do were for our own good. When we came to understand that they had our best interest at heart, we gained a better sense of why they enforced obedience on us. That's when the hesitation stopped. That's when the demands for reasons stopped. It came to the point that all we wanted to do was submit to our parents' authority the first time they told us.

A famous preacher once said, "Procrastination is disobedience in slow motion." When we fail to respond to God's Word when He instructs us to do something, it is disobedience no matter how we try to twist it. Obedience is instant. We hear and we obey by doing. Look at Psalm:

> I pondered the direction of my life, and I turned to follow your laws. I will hurry, without delay, to obey your commands. Evil people try to drag me into sin, but I am firmly

anchored to your instructions (Psalm 160:59-61, New Living Translation).

We shared with you earlier how both of us served in the military and how obeying commands was imperative for our service. In the verse above, we clearly see that obedience is not procrastinated in any way. Just as we are expected to obey our parents without haste when we are children, likewise, we as children of God are expected to obey our Heavenly Father without delay when He tells us to do something.

We know that some people find it difficult to obey authority, especially God's authority. There is a parable in the Bible that Jesus tells about two sons. He explains the importance of being quick to obey authority. Let's look at Matthew:

> But what think ye? A certain man had two sons; and he came to the first, and said, Son, go work to day in my vineyard. He answered and said, I will not: but afterward he repented, and went. And he came to the second, and said likewise. And he answered and said, I go, sir: and went not. Whether of them twain did the will of his father? They say unto him, The first. Jesus saith unto them, Verily I say unto you, That the publicans and the harlots go into the kingdom of God before you. (Matthew 21:28-31).

In the verses above we see a son being disobedient to do what his father had told him to, but later decided to be obedient and do what his father had told him. In contrast, the other son said he would obey his father, but changed his mind and disobeyed. Let's read a little further in Matthew:

> For John came unto you in the way of righteousness, and ye believed him not: but the publicans and the harlots believed him: and ye, when ye had seen it, repented not afterward, that ye might believe him (Matthew 21:32).

One father gave the same request to two different sons, but their responses were different. When Jesus asked the group which son obeyed the will of his father, they said the first son had. Then, Jesus used that example to remind them how they too claimed to obey God in their words but didn't in their actions. Even when the so-called leaders saw the publicans and prostitutes repent and believe, they still refused to obey, repent, and believe. Lips that say, "Amen," mean nothing without hands and feet backing them up.

The point being, when we say we are going to obey God's authority and then don't do it, it's disobedience. Likewise, when we say that we are *not* going to obey God's authority, but later change our mind and obey Him, it is still obedience. We are just slow at doing it.

We believe that most people are like the second son. We commit and promise to do things that we know are the right things to do, but for whatever reason, we never get around to doing them. Look at verse 29 again:

> And he answered, 'I will not'; but afterward he regretted it and changed his mind and went (Matthew 21:29, Amplified Bible).

The King James version says, "He repented." Here, the Amplified Bible says, "He regretted." The first son regretted that he disobeyed his father by telling him "No," and so he changed his mind. "Why did he change his mind?" someone might ask. He changed his mind because after he had told his father "No," he quickly realized that he was wrong and had disobeyed his father. That's why he repented and did what he knew was the right thing to do. The first son was sorry for not doing what his father asked him to do at the time of the asking.

Jesus compares the first son with the corrupt tax collectors and prostitutes. Even after we have disobeyed God in the past, because we now choose to obey God's Word and repent, we are deemed as righteous in Jesus' eyes. Nevertheless, when we know that we have disobeyed God and choose not to repent and obey, we are deemed as unrighteous in the eyes of Jesus.

The second son is compared to the Pharisees and the religious leaders. They say the right things. They promise they will obey but never do. There is no sorrow; therefore, there is no repentance. Both sons disobeyed their father. The first son disobeyed his father with his words, and the second son disobeyed his father through his actions.

Jesus even said that everyone who calls Him "Lord" would not obey and do what He says to do (Matthew 7:21). Just *saying* what we are going to do but never following up our words with actions will disqualify us from the blessings of God. We must be quick to obey the commandments of Jesus in our doing, not just with our words. As the saying goes, "Most things are easier said than done."

We want God to obey us, but when it comes to obeying Him, we make excuses and come up with all types of reasons why our disobedience towards Him is valid. When God tells us to do something, it's not our responsibility to try and figure out how we are going to carry it out. Our responsibility is to step out in obedience and allow God to work through us to bring it to pass.

Chapter VIII
Obedience Brings Prosperity

We have already seen the benefits when we obey God's Word and the harm it brings when we disobey His Word. When we obey God, we receive His promise of blessings in our life. One of those blessings is prosperity. Look at Proverbs:

> Those who listen to instruction will prosper;
> those who trust the Lord will be joyful
> (Proverbs 16:20, New Living Translation).

God has told us that He would bless the works of our hands (Psalm 128:2; Deuteronomy 2:7). While blessing is God's favor and protection, prosperity is more than just receiving a blessing. With prosperity comes the entire package deal from God.

According to Vines' Complete Expository Dictionary, the word "prosper" means "to help on one's way." We don't know about you, but we have discovered that we need help living this Christian life. We determined a long time ago that we couldn't do it alone. But notice how the verse is worded: "Those who listen." You could say, "Those who listen and obey."

We already know that listening to God's Word is only half of what He has told us to do (Romans 10:17). To make the circle complete, we must also be obedient to hear His Word. Listening and hearing can be mistaken for the same thing, but they are two different acts of obedience. We wanted to show the Scripture above from Proverbs, because we wanted to show the contrast between the words "listen" and "hear." Let's explore the meaning of those two words.

Let's start with the word "listen." The American Dictionary of The English Language, Noah Webster 1828, defines the word "listen" as: to hearken; to give ear to; and to attend closely with a view to hear. It also gives this definition: to obey; to yield to advice; and to follow admonition. In that same dictionary, the definition for the word "hear" is: to attend; to listen; and to obey. Another one is: to attend to the facts, evidence, and arguments in a cause between parties.

It's ironic that the word "listen" only appears in the Scriptures one time, which is found in Isaiah 49:1. But when it comes to the word "hear," it is recorded 39 times, the word "heard" is 35 times, and the word "hearing" 39 times. That's a combined total of 113 times. Even though the word "listen" only appears once in the Bible, it is equally important to obeying the Word of God. They are both required to prosper. One cannot hear unless they first listen. Let me explain.

Normally, when people want to get your attention, they will say something like, "Listen to me" or "Look at me." Very seldom will they say, "Hear me." They all elicit the same response—to make you notice and regard what is being said. Listening is something that is done deliberately. It is an intentional act. We listen to music. We listen to people talk. We listen to the sound of nature. We listen because we desire too. While listening is an act on our part, hearing is what's taking place as we listen. Hearing could be considered an outcome. In other words, what happens when we hear something or someone speak? What is our reaction to hearing? From a spiritual perspective, how we hear the

Word of God should influence the way we live. How does it change our life? Does what we hear move us to do something better than before we heard?

We believe this is why Jesus put so much emphasis on hearing. Jesus knows that what we hear will be what will prosper us. He knows that as we hear the Word of God and obey what we hear, it has the power to prosper us. Look at Joshua:

> This book of the law shall not depart out of thy mouth; but thou shalt meditate therein day and night, that thou mayest observe to do according to all that is written therein: for then thou shalt make thy way prosperous, and then thou shalt have good success (Joshua 1:8).

The word "meditate" means: to care for; and to attend to in the Vine's Complete Expository Dictionary. We see the word "attend" used there, which we also saw used in the meaning of both "listen" and "hear." So, we can conclude from Joshua that if we obey God's Word both day and night and are obedient to do what it says, then our way of life will be prosperous.

Let's look at what Jesus has to say about hearing. On three different occasions, Jesus ended His teachings by saying: "He that hath ears to hear, let him hear." We find it in Matthew 11, when Jesus was speaking about John the Baptist. In Mark 4, Jesus is teaching on the sowing of the Word. In that same chapter of Mark, Jesus also teaches that how we *hear* the Word and what we do with it will be manifested in our lives. In Luke 14, Jesus taught on several things, but the last thing He taught in that chapter was counting the cost before building a house.

Jesus even warns us about what we *hear* (Mark 4:24). Why would Jesus be concerned about what we hear if it was not critical to our way of living? Jesus knows that what we hear has the power to change our lives for the better. He knows that if we hear His teachings and obey them, they have the power to prosper our lives in every area.

In Revelation 2-3, John recorded what Jesus showed him about the seven churches. After Jesus was finished talking with John about each church, He ended His speech the words, "He that hath an ear, let him hear what the Spirit saith unto the churches." Jesus said if you have an ear, *hear* what the Spirit is saying. He didn't say if you have an ear *listen* to what the Spirit is saying. Jesus is inviting everyone who has ears to hear His instructions and warnings. Jesus is pleading with them to obey what they are hearing.

In Joshua 1:8, the phrase "observe to do according," is an interesting thought. We have read this verse many, many times. But for some reason, when we were reading it this time, this phrase stood out to us. The phrase "observe to do according" could be translated "observe to obey according." In other words, if we observe to obey every instruction in the Bible, it will make our way prosper, and we will be successful. Obedience brings about both spiritual and material wealth, which flows from God's blessing.

In Joshua 1:7, the Good News Translation, the Lord commanded Joshua to obey the whole law of the Bible. That includes everything written from Genesis to Revelation. In that same translation, the phrase "And make sure that you obey everything written in it" commanded Joshua to study the Word of God both day and night to make sure he obeyed everything he read. So like Joshua, we are not only commanded to read the entire Bible, but we are also told to obey everything we read in it.

When we hear the word "prosper," we most often associate it with finances. Finance is just one of the blessings that obedience will bring. Prosperity actually covers a wide range of blessings. When we *hear* the word "prosper," we must *hear* it in the way Jesus instructs us to *hear* it. If we *hear* it in the natural sense, we will only think in the natural sense—money. But if we *hear* the word "prosper" in the spiritual sense, we will think of prosperity in every area of our life. I heard someone say that to prosper means to do better in every area of your life.

There is a verse in the Old Testament that most Christians are very familiar with. In our household, it is quoted quite often. Look at Jeremiah:

> For I know the thoughts that I think toward
> you, saith the Lord, thoughts of peace, and
> not of evil, to give you an expected end
> (Jeremiah 29:11).

We are forever on God's mind. He is constantly thinking about ways to manifest His blessings in our lives. Let's look at this verse from another translation:

> For I know the plans I have for you," declares
> the Lord, "plans to prosper you and not to
> harm you, plans to give you hope and a
> future (Jeremiah 29:11, New International
> Version).

We can see from both translations that God's plan for us is to do good in every area of our life. But even though this is His plan, there is one common denominator that will hinder, slow down, or stop His plan—disobedience. There is one more Scripture we want to look at before moving on. Look at 3 John:

> Beloved, I wish above all things that thou mayest prosper and be in health, even as thy soul prospereth (3 John 1:2).

God want us to prosper in mind, soul, body, and spirit. He didn't leave out any area of our life. But this prosperity will only happen when we are obedient to His Word.

We have talked about listening and hearing God's Word and how they both work in helping us receive God's blessings as we are obedient to His Word. But there is another step, if you will, to being obedient, and that is *doing* His Word. If we only listen and hear God's Word without putting it into practice, we are just a human with a lot of Bible knowledge and no wisdom to execute a single word of it. Likewise, if we go about doing but apart from His Word, then we are always busy, but going nowhere and accomplishing nothing for God. Hearing God's Word and doing God's Word work together like cotton and the color white.

The Bible tells us if we think that we can hear the Word of God and not follow up with action, then we are deceiving ourselves (James 1:22). The doing is a major piece of the puzzle to receiving God's blessings. Let's take a closer look at the next two verses of James:

> For if any be a hearer of the word, and not a doer, he is like unto a man beholding his

natural face in a glass: For he beholdeth himself, and goeth his way, and straightway forgetteth what manner of man he was (James 1:23-24).

Reading your Bible is good, and you should read it daily. But just reading your Bible will have little or no positive effect on your overall way of living. Furthermore, to be a hearer only and not a doer is like looking at yourself in a mirror, then after some time has passed, you forget what you look like. Looking into the mirror shows what you really look like, but it will never change what you look like. What you see in the mirror will only expose what you might want to change or work on. Likewise, listening and hearing God's Word will only bring the flaws, shortcomings, and sin to our attention. It is doing something about what is exposed that matters. This is true obedience at its core. We listen, we hear, and then we do. It is those who accept the authority of the written Word and what it says about them, then do what it says, that will prosper.

Chapter IX
Obedience Requires Focus

Staying focused on God's Word requires obedience to His Word. We believe that one way of achieving this focus is to be obedient to pray. Praying is a major way of communicating with God. It not the only way, but many times God speaks to us while we are in prayer. When we find ourselves waiting on God to answer a prayer is often when we are most susceptible to attacks of the enemy. The waiting period is not the time to quit or slack off from praying. It's the time to dig in our spiritual heels and stay obedient in prayer. Sometimes staying focused and obedient to praying can be painful and stretch us to the point where it doesn't feel good.

Even in our own life, we find it difficult at times to stay focused on prayer. But we have come to understand that it is not prayer itself that is so difficult to do, it's the obedience to do it. Sometimes, we are not focused on prayer simply because we get tired and lazy. Focused prayer takes effort and tweaking, but it starts with obedience. The great theologian and pastor Martyn Lloyd-Jones said this about prayer:

> When a man is speaking to God he is at his very acme. It is the highest activity of the human soul, and therefore it is at the same time the ultimate test of a man's true spiritual condition. There is nothing that tells the truth about us as Christian people so much as our prayer life.

This is a powerful statement, and true. The great Apostle Paul knew something about staying obedient to focused prayer. In the book of Romans Paul said, "Now I beseech you, brethren, for the Lord Jesus Christ's sake, and for the love of the Spirit, that ye strive together with me in your prayers to God for me" (Romans 15:30). Paul knew the challenge of remaining obedient to focused prayer. He used the word "strive" to communicate to the Gentiles the difficulty they would experience in praying for him.

Paul is telling them that they must try hard to enter in to and stay in focused prayer for him. Paul knew that this effort would require obedience to praying for him. We want to look at the above verse from a different translation.

> I appeal to you [I entreat you], brethren, for the sake of our Lord Jesus Christ and by the love [given by] the Spirit, to unite with me in earnest wrestling in prayer to God in my behalf (Romans 15:29-31, Amplified Bible, Classic Edition).

In this translation, the word "wrestling" is used. Perhaps we can relate more to wrestling in prayer than we can to striving in prayer. We are not saying that one is better or worse than the other. They both give us a snapshot of what an obedient, focused prayer life looks like. It's not that we strive, wrestle, or struggle with people, but with demonic spirits. Look at Ephesians:

> [For] Our ·fight [conflict; struggle] is not against·people on earth [L flesh and blood] but against the rulers and authorities and the ·powers [or cosmic powers/rulers] of this ·world's darkness [L darkness], against the

spiritual powers of evil in the heavenly ·world [realm; places] (Ephesians 6:12, Expanded Bible).

The King James translation uses the word "wrestle." We see that the Expanded Bible uses the words "fight," "conflict," and "struggle" to explain what one will experience when engaged in obedient, focused prayer. If you are a praying person, and we hope that you are, then you know that staying focused in prayer can sometimes be a fight and a struggle. We often find ourselves in conflict with these demonic powers and must fight to stay focused. This is when our obedience to prayer must be on display. If we are not obedient to what the Bible tells us about praying always with all prayer and supplication in the Spirit (Ephesians 6:18), praying without ceasing (1 Thessalonians 5:17), and praying one for another (James 5:16), then we will never stay focused on the things that we know are right.

But sometimes, there is another factor in play—the flesh. It's not that we don't have the desire or want to pray. It's that our flesh wants to do something else. The devil never wants us to pray, so we can conclude that even when there is a fight, conflict, or struggle with our flesh, its origin is demonic activity. The Bible tells us that our spirit is always willing to pray, but it's our flesh that we must deal with (Matthew 26:41). Satan likes nothing more than to steer us away from obedient, focused prayer.

Brenda: I shared earlier with you that one of my responsibilities in finding a wheelchair for my sister was to pray. This was prayer that was inspired by the Holy Spirit. I know some would say, "All prayer should be inspired by the Holy Spirit." We would partly agree with you. But some prayers are inspired by the circumstances in our life. And I will add that these types of prayers often don't take much focus to carry out but do require obedience to do it.

For many years, I worked in Special Education. I had been employed at my current school for over twenty years, working in the same position. After working under the same principal for several years, a new principal took over the school. After being principal for a few years, she decided to move me to a lower-functioning group of children. These children were nonverbal and could not do anything independently. I had worked with special needs children like this before, so it was nothing new to me.

When I got the news that I was being moved, I became upset and nearly lost my focus on the bigger picture. It was very painful and stressful compared to the higher-functioning children that I had been working with. I found myself focusing on things that were not good. I knew what I was feeling was not right, and I had to do something about it. After praying and renewing my mind about the move, I developed a new attitude. Prayer changed my whole perspective about how I was feeling. I went into that classroom with the right attitude, and every one of those children met their Individual Education Plan (IEP) goals successfully that year. It was one of my best years at that school. My supervisor said she had never seen that happen before.

Those children got what they deserved—someone to love and instruct them, and I was blessed beyond measure. Our obedience will not only change our lives, but it will also change the lives of others. Now that I am retired, I look back at that situation and imagine how it could have turned out if

I had decided to be disobedient and refuse to make the move to another classroom. When Jesus was praying in the Garden of Gethsemane, He could have easily disobeyed the Father's *will* and focused on something else. But He knew His reason for being there and submitted Himself to the Father. Jesus carried out the Father's *will* through His obedience to Him because He stayed focused in prayer and on what the Father wanted. Even if we are not inspired to pray, we can do it through our obedience. Jesus is a great example.

Sometimes, we find ourselves in situations where all we know to do is to pray. During these times, nothing and no one must tell us or encourage us to pray; we just know it's the right thing to do. When we desire to see change, we pray. We could easily wallow in our confusions, struggles, and mishaps and do nothing but accept our fate, but we know that with God all things are possible (Matthew 12:26). The connection between us and God is through our prayer.

Chapter X
Humbleness Leads to Obedience

> And being found in fashion as a man, he humbled himself, and became obedient unto death, even the death of the cross (Philippians 2:8).

It takes a strong person to humble himself. When we humble ourselves, we choose to take a lower place. We find this throughout Scripture. In Luke 1:52, we read about how Jesus humbled Himself to a lower degree just to exalt another person. In Romans 12:16, we are told to do things for others, people who have no ability to return the favor, and join with them in solving their problems so that we stay humble. We are also instructed to be humble in spirit (Matthew 11:29). Lastly, the Bible tells us that when we humble ourselves before the Lord, He will exalt us (James 4:10). When we humble ourselves unto the Lord, we create a condition where it is easier to obey Him, which leads to receiving His blessings.

Jesus, the Head of the Church, the Savior of the world, the Son of God, and the second Person of the Trinity, reduced Himself to a condition that would benefit mankind, and He did it for 33+ years until the time of His death. It is noteworthy to understand that Jesus did not humble Himself to obedience in His position as the Anointed One of God, but as a human man of flesh.

Even though Jesus was the Son of God, the Anointed One, He humbled Himself and took the form of man. His humbleness led Him to obedience to do the Father's *will*.

The Scripture states that Jesus emptied Himself and took on the form of a servant (Philippians 2:7, Modern English Version). When Jesus became a man, he "emptied Himself," or laid aside the characteristics of His glory; He humbled Himself. We believe that Jesus' obedience to the Father depended upon His humbleness to serve others.

To obey God, we must first empty ourselves of our way of thinking and the world's way of doing things. Just as Jesus did not occupy Himself with the things of the world but focused on the *will* of the Father to obedience, likewise, we as children of God must purposely empty ourselves of the world's standard of living and become a servant of God unto obedience. Jesus was a Divine Person appearing in the form of God, but did not declare Himself as such, humbling Himself to a state of obedience instead.

In Philippians 2:8, the phrase, "obedient unto death" says it all about Jesus' obedience unto the Father. Jesus was *willing* to obey the Father at the expense of His life. When Jesus was in the garden praying before He was taken to face His death, His words to the Father were, "Thy will be done" (Mathhew 26:42).

If only we as Christians could be half as obedient to God as Jesus was. Even though we are told to imitate Jesus, we fall short in obedience. Look at Ephesians:

> Imitate God, therefore, in everything you do because you are his dear children. Live a life filled with love, following the example of Christ (Ephesians 5:1-2, New Living Translation).

When we humble ourselves in obedience to God when we are going through tough times, it brings peace and a sense of joy. When we live in full obedience towards God, we will experience the manifestation of His promises. Kenneth E. Hagin said this, "Whatever God has called you to do—whatever He's gifted and endued you by the Holy Spirit to accomplish—He hasn't changed His mind about it. One day you will have to give an account of what you did with that calling. Obedience to God's call will bring blessing and satisfaction to your life." We want the blessings of God, but many times we don't want to humble ourselves to obey Him in following His instructions.

"Humility is the key to experiencing God's power." Jim Cymbala.

Chapter XI
Obedience Prevents Us from Becoming Spiritually Hungry

As we have already learned, it's important to know what the Bible says. But is more important to do what the Bible says. We can't put the horse before the cart, so we must know the Word before we can obey the Word. When we know the Word and respond to it in obedience, it keeps us spiritually fed.

Let us give you an illustration. When we are accustomed to doing something repeatedly, we gain a sense of familiarity with it. So we have no problem with knowing what to do, and we also know how we should respond to what we are told to do. This reminds us of the preparatory command and the execution command. When we are given the command to do something, we must follow it up with action. Knowing God's Word and doing what it tells us to do helps keep us full of His desire for our lives. Look at Deuteronomy:

> Always remember these commands that I give you today. Be sure to teach them to your children. Talk about these commands when you sit in your house and when you walk on the road. Talk about them when you lie down and when you get up. Tie them on your hands and wear them on your foreheads to help you remember my teachings (Deuteronomy 6:6-8, Easy-to-Read Version).

Reading and meditating on God's Word is to be a daily routine. The Bible instructs us to live by every Word that we find in the Bible (Luke 4:4). Every command that we find in the Word of God is there to keep us spiritually fed. But we can't just know the Word and not do the Word. This is the responsibility of the parents. Training and instructing our children in the Bible is not the responsibility of the government or schools. Furthermore, it's not the responsibility of the church. The church is there to support the parents, but it is the parents, grandparents, and the like who have the primary responsibility for training a child in the way they should go (Proverbs 22:6).

Just having knowledge of the Word with no application of it is like putting food into your mouth without chewing and swallowing it. That does the physical body no benefit. Likewise, just knowing the Word but failing to do it does our spirit man no benefit.

Someone once said, "It's easier to build a boy than to mend a man." Teaching our boys and girls to know the Word of God and then obey it will keep them spiritually fed and never spiritually hungry.

Conclusion

As we bring this book to a close, the things we have discussed will forever remain. We live our everyday lives obeying or disobeying. Our quality of life can be measured by our willingness to do things God's way or by doing them our way. Consider Mary, the mother of Jesus. She was unfaltering in her obedience to the angel of God. Because she was obedient and submitted to God's plan, she is known as the virgin girl who gave birth to the Savior of the world. If she had been disobedient, God would have been forced to ask another woman to carry out His redemptive plan for humanity. And what about Joseph? He was obedient to God's plan too. The angel of God instructed him not to put Mary away as he had planned, and he agreed not to, which was instrumental in the birth of Jesus (Matthew 1:20). Mary and Joseph are a perfect example of God's way always being the better way.

In this book, we have shared some of our own personal stories and stories of people from the Bible. The things that we have shared with you are not just for an elite group of people, but for everyone. Obedience to God and His Word is for everyone, especially if we expect to receive His blessings. When we obey the will of God, our lives began to flourish and take on new meanings. John tells us if we do the commandments of Jesus, we will be given access to the tree of life and welcomed to enter His gates (Revelation 22:14).

When we accept Jesus Christ as our Lord and Savior, from that day forward, we are to strive to live a life of obedience to Him and His Word. It is no longer our way of living, but how He said we should live.

We hope and pray that you have been blessed with the things we have shared with you. We pray that you will be a person who submits to God's Word and His way of doing things, even when they seem strange.

Before you can begin to obey, you have to know Jesus. If you don't know Jesus, don't put it off another minute. Today is the day of salvation. Pray the following prayer:

> Dear heavenly Father, I come to You as a sinner. Today, I am asking You to come and live in my heart. I repent of all my sins. I accept You today, Jesus. Thank You for giving me new life and a new nature. Satan, sin, I don't serve you anymore. From this day forward, I will serve You, Jesus Christ. I make Jesus Christ the Lord and Savior of my life. Amen.

Congratulations! You are now part of the family of God. If you prayed this prayer, we know that you meant what you just prayed. Now, the important next steps are that you tell someone that you prayed to ask Jesus to come into your heart, find a Bible-believing church, and read your Bible daily. Your life is about to change for the better.

About the Authors

James and Brenda live in Knoxville, Tennessee. They have been married for nearly 35 years. They are both veterans of the United States Army with over 37 combined years of active-duty service. Both are retired from their local school system, where Brenda worked as a Special Education Teacher's Assistant and James as a school security officer.